STAND UP IN PRAISE TO GOD

PREACHING FOR TODAY

STAND UP
IN PRAISE TO GOD

by

PAUL STROMBERG REES

WM. B. EERDMANS PUBLISHING COMPANY

GRAND RAPIDS, MICHIGAN

Library of Congress Catalog Card Number, 60-53088

Printed in the United States of America
By American Book–Stratford Press, Inc.

To
JULIANNA
My Youngest
Blithe as Shelley's Skylark
Loved by God before she knew it
Loving God and happily knowing it

CONTENTS

PREFACE

THE SERMONS that follow fall into a trinitarian pattern. They are attempts to say things neither novel nor profound, but rather relevant and helpful, about the utterly great God who speaks within and lives above every page of Holy Scripture.

With all the pathetic inadequacies that we preachers forever bring to our task, God must nevertheless be preached in all the mystery of His being and all the range of His action. When this is done, the only worthy response is an adoration touched with rapture and a service motivated by what Franz Lizst once called "the madness and elevation of the Cross."

I shall be grateful if anything in these messages can be used by the Divine Mercy to stimulate precisely this kind of response.

— PAUL S. REES

Minneapolis, Minnesota

I

"GLORY BE TO THE FATHER"

"Father, how wide Thy glory shines,
How high Thy wonders rise!
Known through the earth by thousand signs,
By thousands through the skies."
— Isaac Watts

"For thus saith the high and lofty One that inhabiteth eternity, whose name is Holy; I dwell in the high and holy place, with him also that is of a contrite and humble spirit."

Isaiah 57:15

1

THE MAJESTY AND MERCY OF GOD

HOW do you think of God?

According to a poll that was taken not long ago, described as "the first extensive study of the beliefs and practices of adult Americans," ninety-nine percent of the people believe in God's existence.

But you would get a similar answer if you took a poll in India, where it would come nearer being one hundred percent!

The Hebrews of the Old Testament were very little concerned about the *existence* of God. They took that for granted. Their concern was, as ours should be, with the *character* and the *activities* of God.

Let us not imagine that even among the Hebrews it was always easy for them to hold belief in a God who was at once infinitely good and almighty in power. Even the prophets had their faith tested.

Listen to Isaiah, describing the high-handed wickedness of the people of Judah in a day when they were imitating the worst idolatries and vices of the pagans around them: "Meanwhile the good man dies, and no one heeds it; pious men are perishing, and no one cares" (v. 1, Moffatt).

But move on toward the close of the chapter. The prophet hears God speaking: "Their sins have made me angry for a while, I struck them in my wrath and turned away, and they went on, wilful, rebellious. I marked them . . ." (vv. 17, 18a).

Thus it is driven home to the prophet that if no one else cares, God does!

At the same time, with equal clarity, it was made known to Isaiah that God's moral concern about His creatures takes on more than the color of His anger, more than the form of His punishment. It takes on the character of His pity and saving goodness. At the point where their rebellion ends, He says, "But now I heal them, I will give them rest, and recompense them with all consolation" (v. 18).

So you have in God, says Isaiah, both majesty and mercy, both the terrible and the tender, both loftiness and lowliness. And the summing up of all this is in our text, which Moffatt translates: "For he who is high and uplifted, the Majestic One, he who sits enthroned for evermore, declares, 'I sit on high, enthroned, the Majestic One, and I am with the crushed and humble soul, to revive the spirit of the humble, and to put heart into the crushed.'"

I

Consider for a moment the *majesty* of God.

As you look at it through the prophet's eyes, you see three facets of it: God's *loftiness,* His *unchangeableness,* and His *holiness.*

There's His *loftiness:* "Thus saith the high and lofty One."

The religion of the Bible—whether the Hebrew faith of the Old Testament or the Christian faith of the New—is pitilessly hard on all low and petty views of God. The Bible is forever reminding us that it is no use for us to talk about the God who is *beside* us or *within* us unless we recognize Him as the God who is *above* us.

If there is no God that is above us, then the God we fancy within us or beside us is merely the offshoot of our wishful thinking. The God of Isaiah possesses infinite loftiness. He stands above nature. He stands above humanity. He stands above what is to us the known and the unknown. To borrow St. Paul's phrase, He is "God over all!"

Then there is His *unchangeableness*. This, too, is part of His majesty. Isaiah reports that He "inhabiteth eternity." What a superbly round and eloquent expression is that!

You and I, to a large extent, are prisoners of time and of space. God, on the contrary, is the uncreated Master and Transcender of time and space. We are creatures of calendars and clocks and feet and yards and miles. God is not.

Failure to recognize this lies behind some of the problems that needlessly upset us. We say, for example, "How can God listen to my prayers when thousands of other people are praying to Him at the same moment?"

We ask that question because it is so hard for us even to *think* outside of our prison of time, with its succession of minutes, and of space, with its measurable stages from *here* to *there*. But even we, in certain circumstances, can get above these limitations.

Consider this. On a Fourth of July a friend of mine took me in his plane from a small California town to the airport in San Francisco. The highways were choked with traffic. Thousands of feet above these myriad cars, we could take in, in one

momentary view, a wide expanse of countryside. We could see
the movements of hundreds of cars simultaneously, the directions in which they were travelling, and the towns toward which
or from which they were proceeding. But suppose that suddenly
I had been transferred to one of those cars on the highway. Immediately time and space would take on a decidedly different
meaning for me. Now, in that line of traffic I would be conscious
that our pace had been slowed down to, say, ten miles an hour.
I would be wondering if we were going to "make" that next
green light or be stopped by a red. I would have almost no
knowledge of the total traffic situation in that area of the state.
Getting "above" it in the plane had enabled me, within limits,
to transcend both time and space.

Thus when we ask, "How can God hear thousands of people
praying at the same time?" we are really forgetting that numbers—one, two, three, four—have no such meaning for Him as
they do for us. In His circle of infinity thousands of years in
time or thousands of leagues in space are seen simultaneously.
For He "inhabiteth eternity."

If you want an eloquent echo of Isaiah's eloquent phrase, you
have it in Hebrews 1:10-12, "Thou, Lord, in the beginning
hast laid the foundation of the earth; and the heavens are the
works of thine hands: They shall perish; but thou remainest;
and they all shall wax old as doth a garment; and as a vesture
shalt thou fold them up, and they shall be changed: but thou
art the same, and thy years shall not fail." Majestic in His
everlasting unchangeableness—that is our God!

But He is majestic, also, in *holiness*. "Whose name is holy,"
says Isaiah. Here, let us understand, stands the blazing throne
of all moral reality: God is holy!

Are you in awe of that supreme and solemn fact? I wonder.
Almost everything about our times is against it. This thing-mad

culture of ours, with its blind reliance on man-made contrivances, all the way from Salk vaccine to cyclotrons, knows almost nothing of the dazzling vision of God's eternal holiness.

And some of our religious—yes, even *evangelically* religious —tune smiths have not helped the matter a particle. With popular ballads, such as "Somebody Up There Likes Me," and Saturday-night rally ditties, such as "On the Jericho Road There Is Room for Just Two," nobody is likely to close his eyes and drop his head, smitten down before the sheer, unsullied glory of the absolutely Holy God.

Years ago, Dr. J. H. Jowett wrote, in his book *The Transfigured Church:*

"We leave our places of worship, and no deep and inexpressible wonder sits upon our faces. We can sing these lilting melodies; and when we get out into the streets, our faces are one with the faces of those who have left the theaters and music halls. There is nothing about us to suggest that we have been looking at anything stupendous and overwhelming. Far back in my boyhood I remember an old saint telling me that after some services he liked to make his way home alone, by quiet by-paths, so that the hush of the Almighty might remain on his awed and prostrate soul. That is the element we are losing."

Jowett, I am afraid, would be even more grieved and alarmed if he were to observe us today.

But with this man Isaiah it was different. When the vision of the Holy One seized him, he was shaken by it. "Woe is me!" he cried. "Mine eyes have seen the King, the Lord of hosts" (6:5).

II

And now turn, with the prophet, and consider with astonished gladness the *mercy* of God. The Lord Almighty is revealed through Isaiah as the One who says: "I dwell in the high and holy place, *with him also that is of a contrite and humble spirit.*"

It was hearing this that led one of the old Puritans to exclaim: "God has two thrones, one in the highest heaven and the other in the lowliest heart!"

Right!—but with this unhappy qualification: there are men aplenty whose hearts, being destitute of lowliness, are destitute of God.

There is a sense in which the whole of the Bible is concerned with the fact that the heart of man long ago drove God from His rightful place there. On that inner throne sits now a usurper, a puppet called Self.

Now it is the sheer mercy of God that He has set about to win back that place which belongs to Him in the citadel of man's personality. In the searing flame of His anger and judgment He could have destroyed him. Instead, He embarked on an undertaking that St. Paul once described when he cried, "Not by works of righteousness which we have done, but according to his mercy he saved us, by the washing of regeneration and the renewing of the Holy Ghost" (Titus 3:5).

According to Isaiah, this saving compassion of God is marked by at least three things. For one thing, it is mercy *on conditions.* God comes to dwell "with him that is of a contrite and humble spirit." For "contrite" Moffatt has "crushed." The Hebrew word, which is strong, means *shattered, pulverized.* For the proud man there is no mercy—save that of the long-suffering in which God waits and works for pride to crumble. But to the humble, broken man, whose web of lies about his own goodness has been torn to ribbons, God comes in a merciful bestowal of

His forgiveness and a compassionate release of His presence. "Proud man," said Augustine, "would perish unless a lowly God found him."

Mercy on conditions? Yes.

And, for another thing, mercy *with consequences*. Read it as Moffatt has it in the text: "to revive." Here is the purpose of God's merciful invasion of our lives—"to revive the spirit of the humble, and to put heart into the crushed."

Listen to Martin Luther, while trying vainly to work for his salvation and make himself worthy of God's acceptance by feasts and fasts, by penances and pilgrimages: "I hated God and was angry with Him."

But listen to him later: "When, by the Spirit of God, I understood these words, 'The just shall live by faith,' then I felt born again like a new man. The words that I previously detested I began from that hour to value and to love as the sweetest and most consoling words in the Bible. In very truth, this text was to me the true gate of Paradise!"

That is mercy with consequences—and what consequences!

Mercy on conditions, mercy with consequences, and now, one thing more—and this a very solemn thing—it is mercy or *catastrophe*. I want you to catch the meaning of this sixteenth verse: "I will not afflict for ever, I will not be always wroth; for then man's spirit would give way before me, the very souls that I had made" (Moffatt). If God showed us only the north side of His character and blew upon us only with the wind of His judgment, we should all be doomed. The alternative to His mercy is a holy wrath that would destroy us.

III

Consider, finally, the *mystery* of God's character in which both His majesty and His mercy have their meeting place.

Does Isaiah stop for a long and wordy explanation of how God can be the "high and lofty One that inhabiteth eternity" and at the same time the lowly One who dwells "with him that is of a contrite and humble spirit"? He does not.

For the best of reasons: there is no explanation—none, at any rate, that fits the neat niches of our little minds that are always trying out their puny powers on matters too huge for them.

The Infinite becomes the Intimate. And that is God's nature. The Sovereign becomes the Saviour, the Majestic becomes the Merciful, the Transcendentally Awful becomes the Tenderly Approachable!

And let us not try to juggle the attributes of God in some ingeniously wooden attempt to balance them over against each other, as in the case of teachers who tell us that God's justice cried out for man's doom and His mercy stepped in to plead for man's salvation. God is not an infinite Conflict; He is an infinite Harmony.

Still, in that harmony there are notes and chords whose music is vaster than our poor ears can fully comprehend. Hence St. Paul cries: "Behold therefore the goodness and severity of God!" His gentleness and severity are not a conflict; they are a community. The faith of the Bible holds them together in a high and precious tension within the fullness of God's character.

Gentleness without severity would give us a God who is characterless and mushy. Severity without gentleness would give us a God who is hard and cruel. Both severity and gentleness, both majesty and mercy, are forever woven into the fabric of God's nature.

Those two famous Scottish ministers, Andrew Bonar and Robert McCheyne, once fell to talking about their preaching. McCheyne asked Bonar what his sermon subject had been on the Sunday preceding. Bonar replied that he had preached from the

text "The wicked shall be turned into hell." Instantly Mc-
Cheyne shot back the inquiry: "Were you able to preach it with
tenderness?"

That incident more than hints at the truth I want to bring
out. The crown of God's mercy is the pardoning of our guilt and
the cleansing of our hearts. But let us never forget that, as
Ronald Wallace says in his exposition of the parable of the man
without the wedding garment, "Men are in danger of the
wrath of God precisely at that moment when they are offered
His mercy." And if, permanently refusing that mercy, they are
permanently cut off, God's judgment upon them will be the
judgment of love.

Do you remember how Dante closes *The Divine Comedy?*

> *"I raised my eyes aloft, and I beheld*
> *The scattered chapters of the Universe*
> *Gathered and bound into a single book*
> *By the austere and tender hand of God."*

The poet was also the theologian: austere *and* tender, majestic
and merciful—that is our God forever and ever.

This God has acted in Christ to bring us back from alienation
and loneliness to fellowship in His Kingdom. The question is:
Have we acted, responsively and decisively, to let Him be God
in us?

If we haven't, this is our moment!

2

THE HIDINGS OF GOD

THE purpose of this message can be stated easily and simply. It is the carrying out of the purpose that will be delicate and difficult. As helpfully as I can, I want to talk to people who are perplexed, distressed, perhaps even distracted, by the mysterious aspects of life.

Between our pride and our impatience, we have a hard time with life at those pincer points where we have to live it without understanding. We are like a Somerset Maugham character who bursts out peevishly:

"I'm not prepared to be made a fool of. If life won't fulfill the demands I make on it, then I have no more use for it. It's a dull and stupid play, and it's only a waste of time to sit it out. I want life to be fair. I want life to be brave and honest. I want men to be decent and things to come right in the end. That's not asking too much, is it? Resignation? That's the refuge of the beaten. Keep your resignation. I don't want it. I'm not willing to accept evil and injustice and ugliness. I'm not willing to stand by while the good are punished and the wicked go scot free. If life means that virtue is trampled on and honesty mocked and beauty fouled, then to hell with life!"

Is that not logical talk? In a way, it is. Yet it totally misses the glory of the concealed! It tries to take the mystery out of life. For in the closing words of that angry outburst you have a remarkably accurate description of history's most hallowed hour —Calvary. In the greatest moment of the world's holiest Person "virtue" was "trampled on," and "honesty mocked," and "beauty fouled."

We may as well face it: the glory of concealment is as truly a part of the workings of God as the glory of revelation. He unveils. He just as truly veils. He gives us some clarities. He just as truly permits us to wrestle with obscurities. What is more, we must admit that even *in* His revealings there are hidings—impenetrable depths of mystery.

I

If anyone asks where to look for these hidings of God, the answer is, "Almost anywhere."

Take the *physical world* in which we live and the universe of which it is a part. It is made up of atoms so tiny that we can't see them. These atoms add up to a universe so colossal that we can't imagine its vastness. The nucleus of an atom is itself the center of a miniature universe around which whirl the electrons. The nucleus is two trillion, five hundred billionths of one inch in diameter!

But if that is the mystery of the *little,* what shall we say of the mystery of the *big*? *Life* magazine concluded its amazingly interesting and informative series of studies called "The World We Live In" with a chapter entitled "The Starry Universe." The sun is our nearest star—ninety-three million miles away. Its light, which travels at about six trillion miles a year, reaches us in eight minutes. But light from the next nearest star, Alpha Centauri, takes four and a half years to reach us, notwithstanding its phantom speed.

This, of course, is "old stuff." It has been known for a long time. Here is what is new: since the Palomar telescope came into use recently, the frontiers of the starry heavens have fallen back so far that two billion light-years are required to describe the distance between ourselves and those celestial orbs that come swimming into the astronomer's view. If we want it in the kind of miles we register on our automobile speedometer, we must write down the figure 12 and put twenty-one ciphers behind it.

Now what do scientists think in the presence of these fantastic revelations? Do they feel they now "know it all"? Listen to this from the subtitle of the article I have been referring to: "Beyond our planet with its rich domains of life lies an endless sea of space jeweled with galaxies and cloaked with mysteries man has but begun to fathom."

Or this from the body of the article:

"Yet it is not merely the size of the universe that dismays the cosmologist when he reaches the frontiers of vision two billion light years . . . away. For here he encounters enigmas that warn him not to assume—as man tends to do—that he can apply the simple physical laws that govern his earthly domain to the deeps of space and time. There is evidence that all his systems of measurement break down when he tries to fit them to the exterior vistas of the cosmos. . . .

Staring into the void, he faces concepts like infinity and eternity, where science and imagination stand together on the brink of darkness, and he can perhaps but echo the words of the philosopher Schiller, 'The universe is a thought of God.'"

Ah, yes, "it is the glory of God to conceal a thing"!

Or take the realm of *human personality*. Someone wrote a book on Tibet and called it, *The Last Home of Mystery*. To which Halford Luccock made comment: "Not so. The last home of mystery is not Tibet but the human soul!"

Three thousand years ago, the Hebrew psalmist, impressed with the mystery of himself, cried, "I am fearfully and wonderfully made" (Psalm 139:14). He prayerfully confessed, "Thou hast beset me behind and before, and laid thine hand upon me. Such knowledge is too wonderful for me; it is high, I cannot attain unto it" (vv. 5, 6).

But I can hear some college sophomore say, "That was long before modern psychology and psychiatry went to work on man!" True, but if that remark is intended blithely to imply that Freud and Jung and Adler and Horney and Menninger have driven all mystery from the domain of human personality, then we can only smile at such naïveté.

Reinhold Niebuhr knows his Freud and Jung, yet he does not hesitate to say: "The understanding of ourselves is even more subject to seeing through a glass darkly than the understanding of the world about us." And he adds, "We are a mystery to ourselves in our weakness and our greatness."

Sinners with a capacity for holiness, free and yet fettered, ignorant and still capable of a knowledge that soars into the heights, an invisible battlefield of love and hate, subject to death and yet full of the instinct and fire of immortality—that is the ceaseless mystery which is ourselves. Every ridge of self-understanding we reach shows some further range of mystery that calls for climbing.

In the depths of the human spirit there are the hidings of God.

Or, once more, consider the realm of *life's events and orderings,* which some call "providence" and others the "government of God." Here again some things are known, but beyond the known there are vast stretches of mystery.

We believe that God has something to do with the big events of men and nations, but not with the little details. Or do we? *Are* there any little details? There may be, but who knows for sure where to draw the line between little and big?

On an April night in 1912 the world's greatest ship, the *Titanic,* on her maiden voyage across the North Atlantic, struck an iceberg. The rescue ship that heard her distress signal was the *Carpathia,* many miles away. It took this ship nearly the night long to reach the scene of the disaster and pick up the survivors. But the investigation revealed that another ship, the *California,* was only twelve miles away when the accident occurred. It could have been on the scene in three quarters of an hour or less. Why was it not? Because five minutes before the first SOS went out from the radio room of the *Titanic* the radio operator on the *California,* having grown drowsy, took off his ear phones and fell asleep. Was the removal of those ear phones by a lone man in mid-Atlantic a mere detail or not?

When I was a very young preacher, I journeyed nearly two thousand miles for a few days of special meetings in a Midwestern city. While there, I was invited out to dinner by a couple who had known and admired my father. Living in their home at that time was a young lady who was the sister of my hostess. That young lady today is my wife! Was that dinner invitation a mere detail or not?

One writer has developed the intriguing theory that if Oliver

Cromwell or Abraham Lincoln had been born ten years earlier or ten years later than they were, the probability is that the world would never have heard of either one of them. This author suggests that it was the singular set of circumstances prevailing in England when Cromwell was forty-three and in the United States when Lincoln was forty-five that called forth the gifts and powers of these men. Who knows? However we interpret it, there is mystery. For in the strange unfoldings and turnings of history—whether on the world scale or the scale of your life and mine—there are the hidings of God.

So we might go on. There is mystery everywhere we turn. Everything points to something beyond itself. Till at last we reach the original and overwhelming mystery of all—the being and nature of God! Some such answer as this is required, it seems, if we are to give an honest answer to the question, Where do we encounter God's hidings?

II

Briefly, let me speak to a second question: *How do these divine concealings affect us?*

For some people they are merely *bewildering*. More or less quietly, and with resignation, these people say, "I simply don't understand it," and they try, so far as possible, to keep mystery out of their minds.

For other people these inexplicable aspects of life are *embittering*. They turn to skepticism and cynicism. They say the universe is without soul or purpose and that if people pray, they are simply saying useless words to

> "*The dreaming, dark, dumb Thing*
> *That turns the handle of this idle Show.*"

It is this attitude that led Dr. Elton Trueblood to write: "Millions are fatalistic. They feel utterly powerless in the presence of forces which they can neither understand nor control."

There are others still who, in the presence of the hidings of God, become too *glibly smart*. They appear to know more than they do. It is the ego giving the brush-off to the ultimate mysteriousness of life. It is against this crisp cleverness that the poet Cecil Day Lewis turns loose his irony:

> "God is a proposition
> And we that prove Him are His priests, His chosen.
> From base hypothesis
> Of strata and wind, of stars and tides,
> Watch me construct His universe
> A working model of my majestic notions,
> A sum done in the head.
> Last week I measured the light, His little finger,
> The rest is a matter of time."

Better far to acknowledge mystery than to fancy we can reduce everything to crystalline clarity!

There are still others who see another course than that of mere bewilderment, or bitterness, or over-simplification. Of them I should like to speak as we seek an answer to our third question.

III

What can we constructively do in the presence of these strange hidings of God?

(1) We can let them *humble* us. That is good for us. God

is Creator and we are but the created. Shall the created one complain if he does not understand *all* the mind of the Creator? If you have never seen the giant columns of the Parthenon in Athens, you have at least seen pictures of them. Dr. Henry Churchill King, in one of his books, pictures a tiny insect making its way laboriously up one of those columns, skirting around an extra large pore in the stone. That insect, suggests Dr. King, is as well qualified to judge the architecture of the Parthenon as finite man is qualified to judge the infinitude of God's plans. Isaiah must have thought along similar lines, for he says, in gentle sarcasm, "Who hath directed the Spirit of the Lord, or being his counsellor hath taught him?" (40:13).

Humility accepts mystery without being smothered or soured by it.

(2) Another thing the hidings of God can do for us *is* to *lure* us. The mystery of the stars lures us to the science of astronomy. The mystery of matter lures us to the science of physics. The mystery of the human soul lures us to the study of psychology. The mystery of God lures us to the practice of faith. The mystery of the life beyond the grave lures us to the hope of heaven. In I Corinthians 13 Paul cries out, humbly yet hopefully, "For we only know bit by bit; but when the perfect comes, the imperfect will be superseded. . . . At present we only see the baffling reflections in a mirror, but then it will be face to face" (Moffatt).

Mystery can beat us down, engulfing us with pessimism, or it can spur us on, beckoning us to the day of illumination that is yet to dawn.

(3) Finally, the hidings of God can *test* us. The testing of which I speak is chiefly this: Are we willing, in the midst of the shadows, to follow the light of what *is* revealed?

Consider Jesus Christ and His Cross. It is the ultimate in

mystery. Yet it is the shining of a great light! The Cross does not so much reveal God's *mind*, that is, His infinite intellect, if I may so express it, as it reveals His *heart*. It is God Himself getting through to our hearts, tracking us down with love's relentlessness in our sins, forgiving those sins, shattering the old self-centeredness of us, and putting God at the center of a new life and a new man!

And when we know God Himself as we meet Him and He meets us at the Cross of Christ, we are not worried too much about other matters. Knowing *God* is a greater thing than understanding all His *ways*.

Someone once asked Mrs. Einstein if she understood her famous husband's theory of relativity. "Do you know all about relativity?" queried the friend. Mrs. Einstein smiled, "No, but I know my husband!" Her mind was not as illuminated as his but, knowing *him* as she did, she admired, she loved, she trusted him.

So, with Whittier, we can sing:

> *"Yet, in the maddening maze of things,*
> *And tossed by storm and flood,*
> *To one fixt trust my spirit clings;*
> *I know that God is good!"*

The ever present God

you cant get away from God

*"Whither shall I go from thy spirit? or
whither shall I flee from thy presence?"*
Psalm 139:7

3

THE PRESENCE OF GOD

TWO testimonials are in my mind as I begin this message. The first is by a preacher, the second by an explorer.

Frederick W. Robertson, of Brighton, England, although he died in his prime, has gone down in history as one of the truly great ministers of the English-speaking world. Robertson lived, as many a genius has, a lonely life. He once wrote of himself:

"I shall be alone as my Master was. I am hated by some who loved me once, not for what I do, but for what I think. I have long foreseen it. And, knowing that the Father is with me, I am not afraid to be alone, though, to a man not urgently made, there is some sharpness in the thought. . . . I am alone now and shall be till I die, but I am not afraid to be alone in the majesty of darkness which His presence peoples with a crowd. . . . A sublime feeling of a presence comes about me at times which makes inward solitariness a trifle to talk about."

21

A preacher, in the privacy of his own room, talking of the presence of God!

Here is the other testimony. Sir Ernest Shackleton and his men were once caught amid the frigid wilds of the Antarctic, their ship destroyed, they themselves marooned. Shackleton took two of his men and set out in search of help. Their way was haunted with a thousand slippery hazards. The storms they fought seemed certain to overwhelm them in icy death. Still they staggered on until, near exhaustion and freezing, they reached a haven for which they had desperately prayed. Later, talking it over, one of the men, Worsely by name, turned to Shackleton and said, "Boss, I had a curious feeling that there was another Person with us." To which Shackleton replied, "So had I!"

An explorer—two of them, in fact—talking about the presence of God!

It is all very well to speak poetically about the "footprints" of God. These men had gone beyond that. They, like the psalmist and a host of witnesses in every generation, had found more than God's footprints—they had found *Him*.

Many years ago this country had a vigorous Christian journal called the *Ram's Horn,* edited by one Elijah Brown. In an issue of that paper there appeared this description of God: "God— that Being whose throne is justice, whose atmosphere is love, to whom all time is now, all space is here, and whose only inability is to sin." The presence of *that* God, in His world and in human experience, is a tremendous and inescapable fact. It got hold of the psalmist one day and exploded in his soul. The explosion sent out tongues of light and fire which still may be seen in this amazing composition that we call Psalm 139.

"Whither shall I go from thy spirit?" cried David, "or whither shall I flee from thy presence?"

Noah got drunk

I

In David's contemplation he is occupied, first of all, with what we may call *the searching of God's presence.* "O Lord," he confesses in verse 1, "thou hast searched me, and known me." This thought of God's complete and all-covering knowledge of His creatures is then developed through the five following verses. Listen to Moffatt's way of bringing the original Hebrew across into vivid English: "Thou knowest me sitting or rising, my very thoughts thou readest from afar; walking or resting, I am scanned by thee, and all my life to thee lies open."

David feels that no circumstance, no posture, no shift of time from day to night keeps God from walking into his life and reading the books of his soul.

Then he goes on: "Ere ever a word comes to my tongue, O thou Eternal, 'tis well known to thee; thou art on every side, behind me and before, laying thy hand on me" (vv. 4,5).

Overwhelmed with this vision of the ever-present, all-knowing God, David bows in self-confessed awe: "Such knowledge is too wonderful for me; it is far, far beyond me" (v. 6).

"This psalm begins," says one of our finest expositors, "with perhaps the grandest contemplation of the divine Omniscience that was ever put into words." "Omniscience"—that is the way preachers tend to talk. We lean heavily on the vocabulary of abstraction. "Omniscience" is all right. It is a word that simply means "all-knowledge" or "all-knowing." But David, being a poet and not a parson, would not think of using it. He avoids the abstract and seizes the concrete. He prefers to say: "All my life to thee lies open." And if that is not omniscience, it is at least one corner of it.

Mark another aspect of God's searching, as David pictures it. It is very personal: "O Lord, thou hast searched *me,* and known *me.*" A community canvass was being made. At a certain door the questioner asked the woman who answered his knock what children she had. She began, "Well, there's Willie, and Horace" —only, being Cockney, she said 'Orace—"and Ethel." But the canvasser interrupted, "Never mind names, I just want numbers." Then *she* grew impatient and a bit indignant. "They haven't got numbers," she protested. "Every one of them's got a name." Quite so! They were *her* children. She was *their* mother. They had personalities that spoke with all the eloquence of their individual characteristics. She knew them not by number. but by name.

So God looks upon His human creatures. Why, according to Isaiah He calls even the stars by names. Nor does He do less, but rather more, with John Brown and Ruth Anderson. He knows the very number of their hairs.

God's presence in His world means that you, dear man, or woman, or boy, or girl, *you* are neither too little for His notice or too unworthy for His care. You are under His eye. Never, for one moment, are you anywhere else but under His eye. And if that eye is like a burning-glass to judge and condemn your sin, it is also like a healing ray to bring health to your forgiven and cleansed soul. If in the Old Testament we read, "Thou hast searched *me,* and known *me,*" in the New Testament we read, that He "loved *me,* and gave himself for *me*" (Galatians 2:20).

II

Consider next *the scope of God's presence.* With the question, "Whither shall I flee from thy presence?" David proceeds, in the second division of the psalm, to answer his own query. He summons all the grace of lofty and elegant speech as he cries: "If I ascend up into heaven, thou art there: if I make my bed

in hell, behold, thou art there." Here we have what might be
called the *vertical* extremes of the universe—the heights and the
depths. One is never beyond the upward or the downward reach
of the divine Presence.

Next we have the *horizontal* range of the Presence: "If I take
the wings of the morning, and dwell in the uttermost parts of
the sea; even there shall thy hand lead me, and thy right hand
shall hold me" (vv. 9, 10). God is universal. God is inescapable.
That is the insight that David is sharing with us.

But suppose someone says, "I shall try no longer to run away
from God. I'll remain here until the daylight fades and the night
creeps in. In the dark I'll be really alone." "That," says David,
"will do you no good," for, "if I say, Surely the darkness shall
cover me; even the night shall be light about me." Moffatt's
translation here is tremendous: "If I say, 'The dark will screen
me, night will hide me in its curtains,' yet darkness is not dark
to thee, the night is clear as daylight" (vv. 11, 12).

The story is often told but its innocent irony never loses its
point. It concerns the atheist father who sought to impress upon
his little son the non-existence of God. He wrote on the black-
board: "God is nowhere." But he got the "w" in "where" a bit
close to the "o" in "no." So when he said, "Son, you read it,"
the little fellow read, "God is now here." Out of the mouths
of babes and sucklings—wisdom!

"Whither shall I flee from thy presence?" Nowhere! Flight is
futile. Escape is impossible. Recognition is the only wisdom.
Such is the scope of His presence.

III

Moving on to the third division of the psalm, we find that the
leading thought is that of *the satisfaction of God's presence*. The

section covers verses 13 to 18. Let me give a few samplings from this paragraph, as translated by Moffatt.

Take verse 13: "For thou didst form my being, didst weave me in my mother's womb." Whereupon, in verse 14, David declares, "I praise thee for the awful wonder of my birth; thy work is wonderful."

Have you ever taken time to read up on the wonders of those two mechanisms with which you eat every day, or tie your shoes, or write a letter, or tinker with the jewels in a watch— your hands? Have you ever gone to the *Encyclopaedia Britannica* and turned to the "E" volume, and there read the section on the human eye?

A little left of the center, behind our fence of ribs, we have a small muscle about the size of our fist. It is called the heart. It is our body pump, and blood is its "stock in trade." How much blood does our heart pump every twenty-four hours? Fifty gallons? A hundred? Five hundred? Well, according to Dr. Peter J. Steincrohn in *Forget Your Age,* it is closer to five thousand gallons. It is possible, says Steincrohn, for that little muscle to exert itself sufficiently to pump fifty *tons* of blood between one sunrise and the next. If we live to the age of seventy, this amazing contrivance of nerve and muscle, weighing a little more than half a pound, has ejected not less than 150,000,000 gallons of blood. How can it do it? That is part of the wonder of it. It is so constructed that it can rest without stopping, thanks to the law of rhythm on which it operates. In a lifetime of seventy years our heart spends nearly forty years resting.

Does such astounding ingenuity as this point to the presence of an intelligent, creative Mind in the universe? Or is it smarter to sit on what brains we have in our cranial cavity and parrot the prattle of some pseudo-scientist who says glibly that he can account for the origin of all things by the theory of the "fortuitous concourse of atoms," which is simply high-brow lingo for the word "chance" or "accident"?

Much more satisfying to the poet-king of long ago and, I should like to add, much more satisfying to me who am neither king nor poet, is the view that the presence of the living God in the world explains more things than any other view. And where it doesn't explain them, where in fact it leaves some things still mysterious, it leaves the way open for faith that there *is* an explanation—an explanation that God may some day share with us.

This, I take it, was David's brave and tolerably satisfying conviction when he cried in verse 17, "O God, what mysteries I find in thee! How vast the number of thy purposes! I try to count them—they are more than the sand; I wake from my reverie, and I am still lost in thee."

Edwin Markham has a thoughtful little poem called "Take Your Choice," which, I think, David would have read with relish:

> "On the bough of the rose is the prickling briar;
> The delicate lily must live in the mire;
> The hues of a butterfly go at a breath;
> At the end of the road is the house of death.
>
> "Nay, nay; on the briar is the delicate rose;
> In the mire of the river the lily blows;
> The moth is as fair as the flower of the sod;
> At the end of the road is a door to God!"

IV

Moving ahead with David, we come to a short paragraph which suggests to us *the severity of God's presence.* "Surely thou wilt slay the wicked," we read in verse 19, "depart from me there-fore, ye bloody men."

These "wicked" ones are described thus: "They speak against thee wickedly, and thine enemies take thy name in vain" (v. 20), to which the psalmist adds, in vivid Oriental style, "Do not I hate them, O Lord, that hate thee? and am I not grieved with them that rise up against thee?" (v. 21).

Some people get terribly worried about these harsh-sounding passages in the Psalms. I doubt if our worry is necessary. Are we never moved to pray passionately, for example, against the liquor traffic and the war system? Now, if we were Orientals we would know how difficult it is for one of their mental temper to talk in abstractions. Instead of saying, "God, overthrow the saloon business" we would probably say, "God, smite down the drink merchants," but the meaning would be no different.

David once had a chance to take personal vengeance on Saul, but he deliberately spared the evil king's life. He was no more vengeful than the man who has never prayed in such intense and colorful language as he uses in a few passages in the Psalms.

What this language does is to point pungently to the solemn, Scriptural, and sensible fact that in God there are both mercy and judgment. And it is our attitude and choice that determine which portion shall be ours—the divine grace or the divine wrath.

A college lad, well soaked with religious skepticism, was walking in a garden with a grand old preacher of the South. "Doctor," said he, "I don't understand how a man of your intelligence and learning can be a Christian." The preacher replied, "I think it is a perfectly intelligent thing to be a Christian."

"But the Bible—how can you believe that?" countered the youth.

"Why not?"

"It is full of contradictions."

"Oh," said the preacher, "I wasn't aware of that, and I've been reading it for years. What, for example?"

"Well," said the young man, "doesn't the Bible say that 'God is love'?"

"Yes."

"And doesn't the Bible say that 'God is a consuming fire'?"

"Yes."

"How do you reconcile the two?"

The preacher stopped in the garden path. The day was hot. Someone had torn off a lovely flower and it lay there wilting and fading. The preacher pointed to the flowers that were blooming profusely and said, "Aren't they beautiful? And they owe their beauty to the sun, don't they?"

"Yes," acknowledged the young man, "they do."

"But," said the preacher, "look at this poor flower lying here all wilted and curled. What causes it to wither like this?"

"Why, the sun, sir," said the young man, "the sun does it."

"So," said the preacher, "it is the same sun that feeds and nourishes on the one hand and that withers and kills on the other. That is the way with God. As long as the flower was in right relation to the sun, it flourished; broken off from that relation, it perishes. Thus when you and I are rightly related to God, His love is our life, our salvation, our joy. But when we break away from Him, refuse His love, shut ourselves away from His life, we pass, by necessity, under His judgment and, if we insist on remaining there, we perish."

That young man got an insight into the character of God that sent his doubts flying, and led, before long, to a surrender to Jesus Christ. The severity of God's presence is all there is left to a man when he refuses the mercy of it.

V

And what is there more to say than the thing that David does in fact say as this great psalm comes to a close? We have now *the supplication for God's presence:* "Search me, O God, and know my heart: try me, and know my thoughts: and see if there be any wicked way in me" (Moffatt has it, "see if I am taking a wrong course"), "and lead me in the way everlasting."

Is the presence of God unreal to us? Is the assurance of God's forgiveness and favor unknown to us? Is the claim that our lives can be God-guided and God-controlled a matter of doubt to us?

Then let us remember this: We don't have to struggle and strain to find Him. All we need to do is to put ourselves in the way of His going. He is seeking us. He has come in Christ, and He is on a quest for us.

In revealing Himself God has no favorites but He does have rules. Sunlight, in reflecting itself, has no favorites either, but it has rules. We just can't get the same reflection of sunlight in a dusty mirror as in a clean one.

When we get the point of that simple illustration we will have the reason for this prayer: "Search me, O God, and know my heart. . . . See if there be any wicked way in me." And that carries with it the plea to take away everything in our lives that is displeasing to God.

Let us tell Him so now. Let Him dust off the mirror of our soiled soul. Then the light of His presence will be gloriously reflected. And with Him—God's Christ who is "the same yesterday, and to day, and for ever"—we will be led in the "way everlasting."

II

"AND TO THE SON"

"Dear Son of God, Thy blessed will
Our hearts would own, with saints above;
All life is larger for Thy law,
All service sweeter for Thy love.

"Thy cross our creed! Thy boundless love
A ransomed world at last shall laud,
And crown Thee their eternal King,
O Lord of Glory! Lamb of God!"
— BENJAMIN COPELAND

4

CAN WE REALLY GET AWAY
FROM HIM?

IN the Cathedral of St. John the Divine in New York is a
gallery surrounded by a series of panels. Each panel represents
a Christian century and bears the name of the person who, from
the point of view of Christianity, most profoundly influenced
the life and thought of his century. Concerning some of the
figures that appear in these places of honor there has been sharp
difference of opinion; but when it came to the choice of a name
for the first panel there was instant and complete agreement
among those who were consulted. Who could reasonably question that the most forceful Christian of the first century was the
Apostle Paul?

Who was this man Paul? Was he among those who were
first to recognize the Lordship of Jesus and to believe in Him as
their Savior? Far from it! He was, in fact, violently prejudiced
against Christ and bitterly opposed to the Christian movement.

33

He made it his business to persecute the Christians with that blind zeal which is the child of pride and bigotry.

Then, one memorable day when he was hastening to Damascus to make further trouble for the Christians, he was arrested by a vision of Christ. It was an experience that penetrated to the depths of his being. It transformed Saul of Tarsus from a hater to a lover of the Lord Jesus Christ. The whole thing seemed so sudden, so revolutionary and astonishing, that even the Christians at first hesitated to accept Paul's profession of faith.

In this sermon I want to deal with one feature of Paul's conversion which is probably too often overlooked. It is that feature which comes to light in the words, "It is hard for thee to kick against the goad"—words which came to Paul as a message of reproach from the Christ who appeared to him. We say that Paul's conversion was sudden. So it was. But is it not suggested by these words of the text that for some time, longer or shorter, a conflict had been going on in the soul of this persecuting Pharisee? Is it not suggested that his effort to get rid of Christ was precisely what any man's effort to get rid of Him turns out to be—futile?

It is as though Jesus were saying to this deceived zealot, "Saul, you are trying to do the impossible. In fighting against My followers you are fighting against Me. In fighting against Me you are fighting against truth and reality. In fighting against truth and reality you are fighting against the universe. In fighting against the universe you are fighting against yourself. So your fight ends where it began—with your own wrong, blind, guilty self. Therefore it is time to call a halt and realize the futility of the whole procedure. You have tried to escape Me, but I have caught up with you. In fact I have been ahead of you all the while. I am the Inescapable!"

Suppose we take this as our approach to the conversion-experience of Paul. To what insights does it bring us?

I

For one thing, *Paul found that if he wanted to be set right with God, Jesus was inescapable.*

Take a fresh look at Paul before he surrendered to Christ. Two important and contradictory facts meet in him. First, he was saturated with religion and was living a correct life according to the religious standards of the Pharisees. And second, he was deeply and distressfully conscious that he did *not* have peace with God. Why this contradiction? Where lay the trouble? Let the answer come from Paul's own lips: "By the works of the law shall no flesh be justified."

There were the commandments. Paul faced them. He acknowledged that they were right and holy. He was striving to keep them, but failed. In vain he summoned his will-power. In vain he lashed himself into new resolves. Nor did it do him any good to say, "Ah, I do not commit adultery; I do not worship idols; I do not steal." There was that searching commandment, "Thou shalt not covet." *There* was the rub. Paul was, on his own confession in Romans 7, selfish and grasping. The law defined his sin but was powerless to deliver him from it. The law faced him in his failure but could not forgive him in his guilt.

Roman 7 and Galatians 3 should be read as companion pieces in the Pauline writings. In the Galatian passage there appears that striking figure of speech in which the Apostle says that "the law was our schoolmaster to bring us to Christ, that we might be justified by faith." The practical drift of Paul's reasoning is that the law, or commandment, brings us to Christ not so much by what it does as by what it fails to do. Its relentless condemnation brings us to the place of self-despair. It has laid upon us demands that we have not been able to meet. It threatens us with penalties that we are not able to avert. What shall we do? Where shall we look?

It is exactly at this point of moral extremity that Christ makes His appearance as our Saviour, as the very embodiment of that loving divine favor by which the guilt of our sins is pardoned and the old chain of repeated sinning is broken. "Through this man," cried Paul after his conversion, this Man with a crown of thorns upon His head and the marks of blood upon His broken body, "through this man is preached unto you the forgiveness of sins." Through this Man, Jesus, a soiled conscience is washed clean. Through Him a right relationship with God is assuredly established. Run the world around, and you will find this peace nowhere else. In that sense, surely, Jesus is inescapable.

What Saul of Tarsus discovered long ago we need to discover for ourselves today. The wife of a prosperous farmer was leaving the town hall one night at the close of an evangelistic service. The preacher of the evening, while bidding her good-night, was led to urge upon her the claims of Christ as Saviour. He found that she was honest and humble about the sins of her life, that indeed she was deeply distressed about them. The gift of repentance had come to her, but she needed to realize that the gift of forgiveness was also hers by faith in Christ.

The evangelist turned to the story of the sinful woman who brought her costly ointment as a love-gift to Jesus. In Luke 7:47 he showed her the words of the Saviour: "Her sins, which are many, are forgiven." He asked her to place her finger on the two words "are many."

"Are those words true of *your* sins?" he asked. "They are," was the frank reply.

"Now," said the evangelist, "move your fingers to the next two words." "Are forgiven," she read, and placed her finger upon them.

"Will you not believe," said he, "that these are Christ's words to you?"

Her answer was a brief prayer that she offered as she looked up with closed eyes and trembling lips. She simply told the Lord Jesus Christ that she believed His word and that she would now begin to thank Him for the good news. It was the transaction of a moment, but its effects spread through the whole of her life and continued happily into the years that followed. She was no longer an exile from God. She was spiritually at home. Like Saul of Tarsus, she found that if she wanted to be assured of peace with God, Jesus was inescapable.

II

The "goad" against which Paul found it hard to fight included, I am confident, another factor. It was this: *Paul found that if he wanted to account for the lives of the Christians, Jesus was inescapable.* To be sure, he was trying to convince himself that he did not like these followers of the Nazarene; yet it is a reasonable guess that at that very time he was secretly envious of them. Do we not frequently use fault-finding and even open persecution as a mask to hide the admiration that we inwardly feel for certain persons?

Here were these men and women whose lives were strangely serene amid surroundings that were dreadfully difficult. Paul listened to their testimony, watched their lives, felt curiously uneasy on the inside. Here were men and women who were fairly shouting their happy assurance that at last they had found, in Christ Jesus, the way of life. Paul listened to that note of assurance, he who was so destitute of a sure triumphancy in his soul, and he was annoyed. Here were men and women who returned good for evil, blessing for cursing, love for hate, and who were happy in doing it. Paul was compelled to face these facts which were being lived out with simple eloquence before his eyes, and he was at a loss to explain it.

Of course, he could come out candidly and admit that the quality of their lives sprang from their faith in Jesus and from the fact that His divine life had indeed entered into them, but that would be to give away his own case as a Pharisee. That would never do! So, to compensate for this inner longing to have what the Christians had, he was out to get their scalps. He was set upon stamping out their sect.

That was the road Paul was travelling on the day of his spiritual rebirth—the day of the Damascus road. Dr. T. R. Glover fancies that, as he journeyed, Paul had seen an ox in the field, kicking rebelliously against the pointed goad of the driver, with the result that the poor creature only drew a keener hurt to itself. A few moments later the Vision Splendid burst upon the passionate traveller from Tarsus. As it broke, Paul heard the Voice say, in effect, "You are like that ox, fighting against the inevitable. You are only hurting yourself. Those secret thoughts of yours, those convictions, half-formed, that the Christians are real and right, those desires that will not down and that throbbing of yearning to be like them—those are the proddings of God to bring you face to face with Jesus Christ His Son."

God is never helpless in the business of redeeming men so long as He has some convincing human samples of His grace through whom He can work. Said John Randolph, an early

American statesman, "When I try to make myself an infidel, I fancy I feel the hand of my mother on my head, and her voice sounding in my ear as she taught me to say, 'Our Father which art in heaven.'" You see, John Randolph could not escape Christ as he had seen Him set forth in the beautiful life of his mother.

Dr. Louis Albert Banks tells somewhere of an incident connected with the death of Thaddeus Stevens, a powerful political figure of his day. Stevens received a call by a clergyman who said to him, "It is no idle curiosity that has induced me to come and see you, but a desire to know your sentiments on the subject of religion. Should you die in this attack, what shall we say about your faith in the Bible?"

"The Bible," replied Stevens, raising himself in bed, "the Bible—take that away and there is nothing left."

Pressed with the question of his personal interest and faith in Christ, he said, "I do not profess to have religion in that way, but my old Baptist mother had it, and I believe in my mother." Again we see the same unavoidable challenge: Christ the Inescapable, set forth unforgettably in the character and life of one of His witnesses! This was one of the goads from which St. Paul, in his pre-Christian days, could not shake himself away.

III

Paul found, moreover, that if he wanted to resolve the inner conflicts of his own life, Jesus was inescapable.

Turn to Acts 9 for Luke's account of Paul's conversion. It begins with the words, "And Saul, yet breathing out threatenings and slaughter against the disciples of the Lord, went unto the high priest." Dr. G. Campbell Morgan, in his exposition of this chapter, contends that the little word "yet" signifies something more than mere continuance. It suggests continuance "in spite of something." That something lay within Paul's own soul. What was it?

In Dr. Morgan's view it was this: Paul was a Pharisee. The Pharisees, with all their faults, were what might be called the Puritans within the Judaism of that day. The opposing religious group was called the Sadducees. They were the rationalists within Judaism. They denied the existence of angels, denied the immortality of the soul, denied the resurrection. They were religion-flavored humanists.

Notwithstanding their easy-going liberalism, the Sadducees held vast power at the time when the Christian movement was getting under way. The high priest was a Sadducee. It was the Sadducees and their Greek-speaking sympathizers who led the opposition against Stephen, which finally resulted in the martyrdom of that saintly soul. In the light of these facts we begin to see where Saul of Tarsus is placed. As a loyal Pharisee he is utterly against the Sadducees. He loathes their worldly skepticism around which they have wrapped a mantle of religiousness. Still, they are against Jesus and the whole Jesus-sect. So is he.

Therefore, in desperation, he has made common cause with cunning infidels in order to exterminate these happy, singing, suffering Christians. And all the while something deep and insistent within him is saying, "Saul, what a contradiction you are! What a bundle of inconsistencies! Whatever else these Christians may be, they are free souls; but you are not. They are inwardly rich; you are inwardly poor. Their lives are a unity; your life is a disunity. They have found something that works; you have not. Why not humble yourself and confess it?"

Something like this, we may well believe, was passing through Paul's agitated mind in that hour when the full light of conviction at last broke through, and he became Christ's man.

Somehow in fighting Christ he was fighting against himself. In order to get right with himself it became necessary—inescapably necessary—for him to come to terms with Christ.

Precisely the same thing is true of you and of me. Someone may now be reading this whose inner life is harried and harassed and hectic. No real poise, or balance, or unity, has been yours for a long time—if ever. Now either you do not know about Christ and what it means to receive the life He offers you, or else, knowing about it, you are indifferent or rebellious. Why not face the facts? Your way of living has been tried, and it has failed. It doesn't add up right.

Why? Because when you live against Christ you are living against yourself. The universe backs the Christian way, but it balks at the way of self-centeredness. It is Christ's way that works! That is not theology merely: it is the wisdom of life itself. The way of hate doesn't work: it recoils on the hater. The way of jealousy doesn't work: it takes the sweetness out of the soul, the song from the lips, and the bloom of health from the cheeks. The way of worry doesn't work: it unfits you for the demands of today and paralyzes you as you look at tomorrow.

But love works. Goodwill works. Trust works.

The soul wasn't made for poison; it was made for sweetness. Christ cleanses away the poisons of the soul—the guilt, the fear the bitterness, the fretfulness—and sets life to music by harmonizing it with God. Who wants that harmony? If you are serious, if you mean business, then I say to you, Christ is inescapably the Saviour and friend you need.

IV

Again, *Paul found that if he wanted to face death as serenely as Stephen did, Jesus was inescapable.* No thoughtful student of

Paul's life has ever doubted that the memory of Stephen's martyrdom played an important part in bringing the young Pharisee at last to a self-surrendering faith in Jesus as Christ and Lord.

They stoned Stephen for his Christian faith and testimony, but all they got was his crumpled, broken body. God received his redeemed and regal soul. And as for Saul, who stood there holding the cloaks of the murderers, he got an arrow in his heart that wounded him into the kingdom of Christ.

Do you think that Saul could ever forget the sight of that upturned face of Stephen, which, even his cursing foes had to admit, looked like "the face of an angel"? Do you think that he could forget that prayer of forgiving goodwill that Stephen offered for his killers—"Lord, lay not this sin to their charge"? Do you think that he could forget that last, rapturous testimony that poured from Stephen's lips—"Behold, I see the heavens opened and the Son of man standing at the right hand of God"? Impossible!

Sometimes one hears it said that unbelievers, too, die without fear or trembling. Perhaps they do. Is that all we should ask of a man when he comes to the gates of death? I want to know: Can he die calmly *and* hopefully? Can he die with assurance that he is going out into larger and brighter life? Stephen did, and the vision of that radiant death was like a goad in Paul's memory. It haunted him, prodded him, gave him no rest.

Then, one shining day, rest came. Paul's resistance was broken down. He came to see that instead of getting rid of Jesus, he needed to get rid of himself. Peace with God—how he longed for it! And Christ gave it to him. The happy secret of the lives being lived by these humble Christians—how he yearned for it! Christ gave him that, too. A sense of inner unity, satisfaction, and strength—how desperately he needed *that*. Christ had that for him also. And a serene confidence that death could be met and conquered—how he prayed for such assurance in his own soul! Ah, that, too, he found in Jesus—Jesus, whom he had tried to escape and could not; Jesus, by whom he was mercifully overtaken and made captive for life!

So much for Paul. What about ourselves?

I have said that if we want to be right with God, Jesus is inescapable. He is equally beyond our escape if we are trying to account for the lives of those who are authentically Christian, or if we are keen to resolve the inner conflicts of our own lives, or if we long for the composure that meets death with serene and unshakable hope.

What goads of God may be at work on us today, I do not know. What bitter-sweet proofs we may have had that the "Hound of Heaven," even Christ, through His Holy Spirit, has been pursuing us with love's incredible relentlessness, I cannot say.

Each of us knows. Each must give his answer.

Let the answer be, in *our* case, what it was in Paul's:

"O Christ, You have won! All resistances are broken, all barriers overleaped."

"I am yours—forever!"

*"Ye call me Master and Lord: and ye
say well; for so I am."*

John 13:13

"On his head were many crowns."

Revelation 19:12

5

"CROWN HIM WITH MANY CROWNS"

IT is said of a group of English authors that they sat one day discussing what they would do if certain heroes of history were suddenly to enter the room. What would they do if Horace, or Cicero, or Dante, or Shakespeare were to appear before them, they asked each other in the course of their conversation. Finally someone asked, "What would you do if Jesus were to appear before us?" Charles Lamb was a member of the group. "If Shakespeare," said Lamb, "were to enter this room, I should rise up to do him honor; but if Jesus Christ were to enter, I should fall down and give Him worship."

Charles Lamb expressed it better than we could, but most of us are perfectly sure that his insight was correct. The greatness of men bids us to rise in respect; the greatness of Jesus compels us to kneel in worship. For His was an order and quality of greatness that, while it was throbbingly human, was thrillingly divine. It was the crown of all greatness, and therefore we call Him Lord.

To be sure, this is not the only title that He bears who is our

Leader and Redeemer. He is called "Jesus," meaning Deliverer, or Saviour. He is called "Christ," which is the Greek equivalent of the Hebrew "Messiah," meaning God's Anointed One. He is called "Teacher," "Master," "Son of Man," "Son of God." So varied are the names that have been applied to Him that when the distinguished Professor Warfield of Princeton came to write his three-hundred-page volume, *The Lord of Glory,* he inserted a special index in which he listed more than one hundred and fifty titles that Jesus bears in the pages of the New Testament. Of all these titles the one that speaks of the highest honor and the most authentic deity is the term "Lord." This is particularly true as it is used by the Early Church. Those early Christians, following the lead of the Apostle Paul, were sure that "Jesus Christ is Lord." They frequently gave Him the triple title "the Lord Jesus Christ," in which title, as someone has pointed out, "we have all the values that the intricate creeds of the Church have attempted to state."

We shall see how true this is as we dip into the pages of the New Testament and there behold the many crowns of Lordship Christ wears.

I

To begin with, *look at Jesus in His revelation of truth, and you will see that He wears a crown.* When Jesus began His public ministry, it seems that the first impression He produced upon men was not that of His holiness or of His love. It was rather an impression of authority and mastery in the realm of truth. "And it came to pass," says Matthew, "when Jesus had ended these sayings, the people were astonished at his doctrine: for he taught them as one having authority, and not as the scribes" (7:28, 29). The scribes were echoes; Jesus was a voice. The scribes quoted authorities; Jesus *was* authority. The scribes split hairs on definitions; Jesus swung about and gave directions. The scribes proposed investigations; Jesus offered insights. The scribes laid down minute precepts; Jesus pronounced universal and enduring principles.

With what sureness of touch He laid hold of the things that mean the most to us! Who or what is at the center of the universe? we ask; and Jesus answers, "My father worketh hitherto and I work." What is the relative importance of material and spiritual values? we ask; and Jesus answers, "What shall it profit a man if he gain the whole world, and lose his own soul?" What is life all about, and what should be its aim and goal? we ask; and Jesus answers, "Seek not ye what ye shall eat, or what ye shall drink. . . . For all these things do the nations of the world seek after. . . . But rather seek ye the kingdom of God" (Luke 12:29-31). What does it mean to be really great? we ask; and Jesus answers, "He that would be greatest among you, let him be your servant." If a man die, shall he live again? we ask; and Jesus answers, "I am the resurrection, and the life: he that believeth in me, though he were dead, yet shall he live. . . . In my Father's house are many mansions: if it were not so, I would have told you."

Here, in sentences that are chiselled out of the eternal substance of things, is the King of Truth speaking to us. Here is the one Teacher who needs never to revise His views or correct His utterances. Let education advance as far as it can, Christ will be forever at the head of the parade. No culture outgrows Him. No science discredits Him. No authority supersedes Him. Rodin, the sculptor, declared, "Beyond Phidias art does not progress." Yet Phidias lived more than two thousand years ago. Even more confidently (for some artist might dispute Rodin's contention) we dare to say that beyond Jesus Christ our Lord no interpreter of moral insights and spiritual values will ever go.

Is it not significant that, after twenty centuries of the advance of learning, a leading scholar of our day, Professor Ellwood, the sociologist, should say, "The greatest problem of the future development of religion upon this planet is what shall be done with Jesus and His teachings. . . . We cannot get away from Christ in religion any more than we can get away from Copernicus in astronomy and still remain sound and sane."

Which is just another way of saying that if we will peer carefully through the smoke and haze of these troubled times, we shall see One who, across the ages, wears the crown of truth.

II

Look at Jesus in His redemption by atonement, and you will see that He wears a crown. The phrase we are now to examine occurs in I Corinthians 11:26, where the Apostle Paul speaks of "the Lord's death." "Christ died for our sins" is the more usual way of expressing the fact of His sacrifice for us. Here, however, the emphasis is thrown more sharply on the thought that God Himself passed along the costly way of pain and death in order to reconcile rebellious men unto Himself.

Modern liberal thought has for half a century and more placed man on the escalator of upward progress and has tried to visualize him as some day reaching the top floor of some ideal state, both personally and socially. The New Testament has never supported any such view of man. The Christian revelation does not picture man as rising to the stature of Christ. Instead, it pictures God as descending to the level of man's sinfulness and helplessness in order to lift him up to the stature of Christ

And that means atonement! Atonement means that there is

a barrier between God and man. It means that man's sin has created a rupture, an enmity, a broken harmony. That barrier has two sides. The holiness of God is one side of it. The pride and perverseness of man are the other side. Now when Christ died, crying, "It is finished," it was, as Edwin Lewis has put it, "the most utterly sacrificial deed of which the Creator was capable: it was the cost of satisfying and revealing His own holiness and of making possible the exercise of His grace."

"The Lord's death" means that the barrier is broken down so far as God's holiness is concerned. It means, moreover, that the appeal of a holy and compassionate God for man's surrender and reconciliation has been raised to the highest possible pitch, for certainly if Calvary will not break down a man's pride and shame him into a confession of his meanness, nothing else will.

To state the whole vital matter bluntly, only God can redeem man. He can do it only by means of atonement. Only because Christ is God, the Lord God Almighty clothed in human form, can He make atonement for us and thus become our Saviour. And because He, and He only, has done this, He wears the crown of honor as the one indispensable Redeemer of man. Says ex-humanist D. R. Davies, "So long as a man nurses the belief that he can save himself, salvation will escape him." And it might be added, when he reaches the place where, beaten and humbled, he admits that he *can't* save himself, there will not be half a dozen saviors standing around, waiting to save him. There will be just one, and His name will be Jesus—Jesus Christ our Lord!

> *"He died that we might be forgiven,*
> *He died to make us good,*
> *That we might go at last to heaven,*
> *Saved by His precious blood.*

"There was no other good enough
To pay the price of sin;
He only could unlock the gate
Of heaven, and let us in."

III

Look at Jesus in His ritual of remembrance, and you will see that He wears a crown. Two phrases may be brought together to support this thought. The first is found in I Corinthians 11:20, where the Apostle Paul speaks of "the Lord's supper," and the second is in Revelation 1:10, where the Apostle John speaks of "the Lord's day." Both the ordinance of the Holy Communion and the observance of the Christian Sabbath speak symbolically and systematically of Jesus Christ our Lord. They point to His supreme and kingly place in our remembrance, our reverence, and our adoration.

Of all the great personalities who have ever walked this planet surely Jesus chose the strangest and the most daring ways of getting Himself remembered by posterity. He wrote no biography. He arranged for no granite shaft or bronze tablet to commemorate His career. He formed no organization, not even a church organization as we understand the term. The risky thing He did was to reach out with the hand of His death and claim the simple elements of bread and wine as a sacred festival of communion and to reach out with the hand of His resurrection and to claim the first day of the week as a feast of rest and worship.

Sometimes we are told that the Christian Church missed the way when it allowed a pagan king, Constantine, to change the day of worship from the seventh to the first day of the week. Constantine belonged to the fourth century. A century and a quarter before Constantine's Sabbath law, that towering soul among the early Church Fathers, Tertullian of Carthage, declared, "Though we share with them [the pagans] Sunday, we are not apprehensive lest we be [counted] heathens." Even earlier, A.D. 153, Justin Martyr announced, "Sunday is the day on which we all hold our communion assembly . . . because Jesus Christ our Saviour on that day rose from the dead."

And when I read this testimony to the observance of the first day of the week by the early Christians, I remember that the Master Himself declared, "The Son of man is Lord even of the sabbath day." Since He died and rose again a new memorial has been set up for Him. It is that day of rest and gladness whereon, around this wide world, the friends of Jesus gather to do Him honor: to confess their faith in His Saviourhood, to drink again from His Spirit, to gather strength for His cause, and to sing the praise of His name. By so doing they are saying to Him and to themselves, "This day is Thine and all days are Thine. On *this* one we gather to intensify our consciousness that Thou art the Lord of all our days, world without end."

It is the same with that other dear memorial that we call the Lord's Supper. Here, where faith reaches out to take the broken bread and the poured-out wine, our sense of His presence is vivified and our communion with fellow believers is enriched. Here, too, we realize that all of life must come under the sanctifying mastery of His touch and His Spirit, else it is an offense to the Almighty.

During a Communion service in the Sandwich Islands a native Christian, young in his faith and tender in his spirit, suddenly rose from the Communion rail and hurried back to the rear of the chapel, obviously shaken by some inner struggle. Then he returned and quietly knelt again at the altar. Explaining his strange action, he said, "I saw kneeling by my side the man who in old cannibal days murdered my father, and I had sworn to kill him on sight. Finally, I was able to pray, 'Father, forgive him, for he knew not what he did,' and return to my place."

Ah, world of troubled, hating, strife-torn men, can you name anyone but Jesus who, by such a simple ritual of remembrance, can cleanse the human breast of its deadly poisons? Here, as elsewhere, He is Lord. He wears the crown!

IV

Look at Him and His rule over life, and you will see that He wears a crown. The phrase that confronts us in this connection is from II Timothy 2:24, which in the Authorized Version reads, "the servant of the Lord," but in the Revised Version, "the Lord's servant." The margin, moreover, brings out more of the strength of the original by rendering it "bondservant." The Lord's slave! "That's what I am," says Paul. "That's what you are, Timothy." And that is what all of us Christians are to be.

Try to forget the ugly side of human slavery long enough to let this tremendous truth soak into your inner soul. You can be sure that Paul was not thinking of the marketing of human bodies like chattels or seeing them beaten like beasts by men who were themselves beastly. Here, in the Christian scheme of things, is a slavery which, in place of debasing men, delivers them. Instead of lowering them, it lifts them; instead of enchanting them, it emancipates them.

And it does it by replacing a lower form of slavery by a higher form. The mastery of God's Christ takes over and the mastery of man's self and man's sin is broken. "Ye are not your own," is Paul's ways of putting it. "Ye are bought with a price." God has "delivered us from the kingdom of Satan and translated us into the kingdom of his dear Son."

If you are a changed man today, if you have received Christ as your Saviour, God *has* put you under the kingship of His Son. That is, the claims of Christ upon you extend to every fiber and atom of your being, every relationship and responsibility of your life, every capacity and energy of your personality. The question is: have you *recognized* and *yielded* to such complete lordship as Christ deserves and demands?

Let us stop saying that we can't be, as Christians, what we ought to be. Let us get on with the task of being honest about it. We just aren't quite ready to let go of ourselves and let this Christ of the many crowns walk into every nook and corner of our lives and claim everything for Himself. It may be a tricky temper. It may be an undisciplined, pleasure-loving mind. It may be a smouldering resentment. It may be a fear of unpopularity. It may be an investment of our lives in service to Christ on some foreign field. Whatever it is, let us be evasive no longer. Let us hand all the keys of control over to Jesus Christ, this moment, and discover for ourselves the widest freedom and the wealthiest fruitfulness our redeemed lives have yet known.

> *"I own Thy right*
> *To every service I can pay,*
> *And call it my supreme delight*
> *To hear Thy dictates and obey."*

Put *that* crown upon the brow of your Saviour, I beg you.

V

Finally, *look at Him in His return in glory, and you will see that He wears a crown.*

To the "word" of the Lord, the "death" of the Lord, the

"supper" of the Lord, the "day" of the Lord, and the "servant" of the Lord, we now add a phrase which St. Paul gives us in I Thessalonians 4:15—"the coming of the Lord." The whole passage has a glow for the Christian Church. It speaks of something tremendous that lies beyond this present age, this day of carrying the message of love and salvation to all who will hear and believe, this day of fierce conflict with the powers of darkness that often seem to be in possession of the field but which, without their knowing it, are heading straight for defeat at the hands of God's Christ.

"The Lord himself shall descend from heaven with a shout!" The cranks and the date-fixers and the end-of-the-world prophets have just about driven the masses into a state of cynicism about the teaching of the Bible on the return of Christ—more's the pity! But, all this skepticism and scoffing to the contrary notwithstanding, Christ is coming again.

"The dead in Christ shall rise. . . . we which are alive . . . shall be caught up together with them . . . to meet the Lord in the air."

Therefore, take comfort, says Paul.

Now this is not the whole doctrine of Christ's return, but it is enough to let us know that it is the *Lord* who is coming—the God-Man wrapped in a robe of light and clothed with authority to judge the nations, to cast down Satan, to vindicate the righteous and to bring order and peace to this tortured planet.

Not long ago one of our national weekly magazines carried a poem that might well haunt the thinking of all of us these days, and not least our political leaders. It bears the title, "Stranger at the Peace Table":

> *"There is a Stranger in the council hall*
> *Where nations meet to plan the peace again.*

He sits unnoticed by the farther wall,
His eyes upon the leaders among men.
His ears attend their clearly laid designs
For living in tomorrow's homes and marts,
As though beneath their spoken words and lines
He hears the inner voices of their hearts.

"But when the delegates of all the world
Have cried their million wants, and lists are long,
And after blueprints, charts, and plans are hurled
In varied protest at the core of wrong,
He is our hope; He is the peace we seek.
O listen, world, and let the Stranger speak!"

Will the world listen? Will it let the Stranger speak? If you are expecting me to offer a categorical No, you will be disappointed. Some of us, I fear, are so steel-bound by the pessimism that expects the affairs of society and of the nations to go from bad to worse that we have no place in our Christian thinking for the real, even if limited, impact of Christian forces on business and politics. Why pray, as Paul bids us, for "kings and all who are in high positions, that we may lead a quiet and peaceable life" (I Tim. 2:2), if we do not expect some good results from these intercessions?

I have lived to see the day in my own life when I became thoroughly ashamed of the by-passing of social responsibilities by multitudes of good Christians who feel that *involvement* is worldliness and that *effective* involvement is somehow delaying the worsening of affairs that must precede our Lord's return. To be sure, none of our moral victories in government and business is complete or final. Each is a relative success. Each is a protest against the evil that would devour both the righteous and the godless in society. Each is therefore worthwhile.

Let us try to remember that when we send men to Congress who go as Christians, what they do can never be done as though we all were living in a Christian social order. They must throw their weight where even an inch of progress is a thing for which to be thankful. Their positions are often difficult, their judgments and decisions necessarily marred by relativities and ambiguities, their triumphs always short of what they and we would like to see.

I have come to feel that there is something curiously cowardly in the way masses of evangelical Christians can sit toasting their shins by a winter-night fireplace while they, in smug detachment, toss about airy pronouncements on what ought to be done with Russia, or Red China, or the United Nations, or the size of the defense budget, or the bosses of Big Labor. What would *we* do if we sat in the place of these Christian leaders? And what are we doing, by way of concerned and compassionate involvement in all this since, after all, it is as truly Christian to render to Caesar the things that are his as it is to render to God the things that are His?

To sum up my meaning, I am convinced that far, far more of an impact could be made by our Lord on the social order if His Church took seriously their citizenship responsibilities.

What, then, is the full New Testament perspective on the relationship of Christ the Lord to history and the future? Does what I have just said endanger anyone's faith in the doctrine of the Second Coming, or reduce by one degree the ardor of our hope in that blessed event? Not at all.

If there is a *distorted* pessimism that some premillennialists have displayed, there is in the New Testament a species of pessimism that cannot be explained away. It is not, however, pessimism about the ultimate victory of Christ, the final realization of His purposes. It is the sort of pessimism of which Professor James Stewart is speaking when he says in his recent book *Thine Is The Kingdom:* "It is suggested in the parable of the wheat and the tares that the roots of good and evil are so inextricably intertwined that it will never in this world be possible to separate them out completely; never will you find a field, a culture, a society so fully Christian that the fruit of the Spirit can grow in peace."

What then?

The "Stranger" will speak once more. He spoke at Calvary— in love and judgment. He won at Calvary—the victory over the entire empire of evil. But He is coming again to finalize that victory, to put into effect that judgment. On the ruins of man's futile efforts to govern the world without God, He— this King of kings and Lord of lords—will establish in judgment and mercy His kingdom of righteousness and peace.

Then our dear departed dead will be with us again. Then war's horror will have passed as some ghastly nightmare. Then shall *God's* "brave new world" take noble shape before men's grateful eyes. Then shall go up the shout of hope fulfilled and faith triumphant: "Hallelujah, for the Lord God omnipotent reigneth!"

6

AND DON'T FORGET HIS ANGER!

LET us face it—Jesus was not only capable of anger—there were times when He also displayed it.

Some of the critics of our Lord have sputtered at this, thinking to charge Him with a flaw and to cast a shadow upon the claim of His sinlessness.

Some of the friends of Jesus have been troubled too, though in a different mood and manner. They have found it difficult to reconcile His obvious indignation with His gentleness and self-restraint.

Perhaps we should not be surprised at this—either at the criticism of His foes or the perplexity of His friends. For one thing, all that Christ was, and is, in the total fact of His being, is not easy to grasp, not even by the reverent mind, to say nothing of the irreverent. We so readily form, especially in our childhood, a mental picture of the Master that is a one-sided stereotype. When such a picture, usually of the "gentle Jesus, meek and mild," fills our minds, we find it hard to explain such scalding sentiments and words as, "Woe unto you, scribes and Pharisees, hypocrites! . . . Ye serpents, ye generation of vipers, how can ye escape the damnation of hell?" (Matthew 23:29, 33).

For another thing, we find that, where anger is concerned, the experiences that *we* have had with it make it far from easy to fit it in with the perfection of our Lord's character.

God knows we have had no lack of experience with it. Anger is among the universals in our emotional system. It starts early and spreads wide. Long before any *Christian* management of it comes into play, it has to be curbed or it will spoil the child and devastate the family. Anger is under every roof and out on every street. Few people can make a million, but anybody can "get mad."

What is more, if we are at all reflective we are bound to have noticed that when people are angry they almost invariably make fools of themselves.

Putting all these things together, it is small wonder that the angriness of Jesus, in certain circumstances, presents a problem. "How come?" we ask, in the phraseology of the street.

The first thing I want to suggest is not a direct answer to the problem at all, though I dare to hope that it will have the effect of letting in some light.

I

We are going to take a look at those who were the *objects* of our Lord's indignation and severity.

First, there were the Pharisees. We see them in clear, contemptible colors in the story from which our text derives. It was in the synagogue in Capernaum. The day was the Sabbath. The keen eyes of the Master fell on a poor man with a withered arm. Should not the man be healed, even though such a ministry to his body might violate the letter of the rigid regulations for Sabbath-keeping that the Pharisees so jealously guarded? When they refused, silently and sullenly, to admit that it was better to do good than to do evil on the Sabbath, the Master's eye was suddenly lit with a blaze of anger, in the flame of which He proceeded to make the man whole.

Pharisees, for whom religion had hardened down into rigid restrictions and regulations—these felt the heat of our Lord's aroused displeasure.

Then there were the disciples. Even they sometimes felt the lash of His wrath. Mark, again, is our narrator. In chapter 10 he tells of a day when many parents brought their children to Him for a touch of His hand upon them. The disciples, either out of cold appreciation for children or out of intense anxiety about the Master's time and strength, interefered. They tried to push the parents and their little ones away. It was a breach of love that Jesus could not pass by. As Mark describes it, He "was moved with indignation, and said unto them, 'Suffer the little children to come unto me; forbid them not: for to such belongeth the kingdom of God' " (Mark 10:14, ASV).

Again, there were the money-changers in the temple. God's house of praise and prayer had been turned into man's house of purchase and profit. The angry ardor of our Lord's holy soul laid hold of some thongs used by the cattle drivers and flailed out the greedy profiteers with their animals, leaving behind, on friend and foe, an impression of something flamingly awesome in the character and face of the Galilean. As His disciples reflected on it, the only thing they could think of was a passage from the Psalms: "The zeal of thine house hath eaten me up" (Psalm 69:9)!

Pharisees with their frigid formalism; disciples with their fussy, if brief, self-importance and unconcern about little children; merchandisers who exploited worship for profits— these were the people on whom the anger of Jesus descended.

Does this strike you as being in any way odd? Can you not

think of others who were more wretchedly deserving of His indignation than these? What about the Roman soldiers who kept the Jewish people in what was to them a degrading subjection? If Jesus was ever angry with them, not a hint of it has leaked through into the record.

There was Herod. His life was indecent and cruel. Was there no anger poured on him? None that is reported.

There was Pilate. He was a rogue of a politician, ruthless part of the time, diplomatic part of the time, self-seeking all the time. No anger for him? None.

Or even Judas—Judas the betrayer—no boiling-over of deserved wrath upon him? None.

Strange anger, this! We had better ponder it well. Pharisees, disciples, money-changers—*they* were smitten by it.

II

If these were objects of our Saviour's indignation, what, in the next place, were the *occasions* when His feelings were loosed in severity?

I have already hinted at these matters but I want now to look into them more closely.

Take the case of the Pharisees who sit there scowling in the background of our text. Their dark eyes are saying, "If He heals this man on the Sabbath, we'll make it hot for Him!"

What vexed the soul of Christ was the warped state of mind and the perverted condition of heart that could give petty rules of Sabbath-keeping more importance than the welfare of men. This crippled man could remain crippled all his days so far as they were concerned. All that mattered was the preservation of a man-made tradition of Sabbath-reverence.

Because the ancient law of Israel prohibited the carrying of a needless "burden" on the Sabbath, the Pharisees had forbidden a tailor to have a needle in his pocket on that day, or any person to wear shoes with nails in them! The legal technicalities were everything; the spirit of the law was nothing. This blindness and distortion of mind put a flame in Jesus' eye and drew down hot rebuke from His holy lips.

Do you think that His eye is less flaming or His lips less reproving today? I don't.

When property values are more important to us than human values, when interest in money surpasses interest in men, there is still a searing fire of indignation within Him. I was living in California when that state, many years ago, passed its Exclusion Act. It said, in effect, we do not regard the immigrants of Asia as being worthy of the same treatment we give to Europeans. They are inferiors. We'll shut them out. That will enable our own citizens to make more money, since they will not have to compete with so much low-price labor.

Well, by the time United States citizens have grown gray figuring out their share of the bill for what happened to them after Pearl Harbor perhaps they will be able to tell the world how much money they made on their insult to the Asians.

God, "who maketh his sun to rise on the evil and on the good, and sendeth rain on the just and on the unjust," has revealed in His Son a burning anger against the inhumanity of man to man. And it is all the worse when it is "doctored up" into something like piety.

Or, take the case of the disciples who interfered with the little children when they flocked around the blessed Master. Let us concede that these men meant well. They were nevertheless far out of line with the mind of Jesus. He was indignant with them for even imagining that He did not want to be bothered with women and their little children. The worth of a child—

how could they discount that? How could they be in such a fog about it?

Maybe we had better give the question another pitch: How can *we* be so careless about getting our children to Christ? How can we be so complacent about the swift breakdown of marriage loyalties and the resulting damage to the emotions of our children?

How can we be so erratic and irrational in our treatment of our own children—part of the time indulgent, part of the time cruel—that the terrified creatures know not what to expect of us?

How can we deceive ourselves into thinking that we can rear our children well by proxy? Between the day nursery, the public schools, the movies, the comics at the corner drugstore, the alley gang or even the Boy Scouts, the lad is all taken care of, while *you,* father, take it easy at the club or raise the glass in the tavern.

How can we be so content to let the beer and liquor industry, through television and magazines, make our homes the dumping ground for their "Madison Avenue" camouflaged but none the less poisonous products?

How can we rest so quietly while millions of America's children grow up in empty-minded ignorance of the Bible and empty-hearted ignorance of the way to new life in Jesus Christ our Lord?

Or take the case of those money changers in the temple. They drew the holy ire of the Son of God because they made a financially profitable traffic out of the sanctities and spiritualities of the temple. They made religion serve their own greedy ends and not the purposes of God. That was both selfish and hypocritical.

And hypocrisy, let us never forget, struck from Jesus the

spark of such angry protest and rebuke as to make one shudder in its presence. Still, there was the churchman, of whom a distinguished friend of mine told me, who in his dying hours was covered with remorse when to a brother-minister he confessed, "I have used the offices of the church as steppingstones to gratify my own ambitions." Had he no stinging sense that the anger of His Lord was kindled against Him while he did it?

These are the evils that ignite anger in Christ: the warped mind that rates religious form above the welfare of needy men, the preoccupation with other things that keeps us from bringing little children into the waiting arms of the Saviour, the self-centeredness that turns the church into an "accommodation train" on which we ride to the realization of our own egoistic ends.

III

Let me close by gathering up certain *observations* on the anger of Jesus that, in part, grow out of what has been already said and, for the rest, spring from our knowledge of the Bible's account of Him. I shall name three.

(1) *Christ was never angry for personal or self-regarding reasons.* Therein may be seen immediately the difference between His anger and the kind so common among us.

Was He angry when He was personally insulted? Never. When He was falsely accused and slandered? Never. When they spit in His face? No. When they plucked at His beard? No. When they mocked Him as a make-believe king? No. When they whipped Him with a scourge? No. When they nailed Him to a cross? No. Not a trace of it!

Our stupid anger is usually shot through with selfishness or occasioned by pettiness as when somebody knocks our hat off, a motorist cuts in ahead of us, a bus driver fails to stop for us, a clerk behind the counter doesn't please us, a member of the family contradicts us.

As Dr. Charles Jefferson, of Broadway Tabernacle fame, once said: "We become indignant over trifles. . . . Ravellings and shavings can set us blazing. But in the presence of gigantic outrages perpetrated on the helpless and the weak, some of us are as calm as a summer morning." To our shame!

(2) That leads readily to my second observation: *The anger of Jesus was not only a sinless but a necessary part of His perfect holiness of character.*

Because Christ's love was so superbly and tenderly shown, a mass of people in our day have run off with the false notion that Jesus was nothing but an incarnation of sentimental good-naturedness. They should learn that the Christ of their soft fancy is not the Christ of the New Testament. Within the perfect tension of His personality Jesus held both gentleness and severity, love and hate, for he who does not nobly hate cannot magnificently love. In the first chapter of Hebrews it is said of Him that he "loved righteousness and hated iniquity." The hatred, the anger, if you please, is but the negative side of His holiness, whereof the positive side is love.

Do you see what that means if you and I have His nature and Spirit in us? It will take the selfishness out of our temper and give it a holy quality. It will increase our capacity to be angry with the giant evils that are blighting bodies and damning souls all around us. When we can put up with these evils tolerantly and calmly, we have parted company with the virile Christ who now and again makes us fall back in awe at His withering indignation.

(3) The final observation is this: *The anger of Jesus was tempered and textured with grief.* The sentence of which our

text is part goes on to say that Jesus "looked round about on them with anger, being grieved at the hardening of their heart."

So there was grief as well as granite in the Master's anger. If His love were all gentleness and no indignation, it would become intolerably soft and mushy. If it were all indignation and no compassion, it would turn out to be hopelessly hard and cruel. It is the blending of both.

Moreover, the indignation, I suspect, actually was for the *hardening of their hearts;* the grief was for *them.* In that compassion lay their hope—and ours, too, if we have the humility to recognize it.

III

"AND TO THE HOLY GHOST"

"Come, Holy Ghost, our hearts inspire,
   Let us Thine influence prove;
Source of the old prophetic fire,
   Fountain of life and love.

"Expand Thy wings, celestial Dove,
   Brood o'er our nature's night;
On our disordered spirits move,
   And let there now be light.

"God, through himself, we then shall know,
   If Thou within us shine;
And sound, with all Thy saints below,
   The depths of love divine."
                    —CHARLES WESLEY

"Nevertheless I tell you the truth; It is expedient for you that I go away: for if I go not away, the Comforter will not come unto you; but if I depart, I will send him unto you."

John 16:7

7

THE HOLY SPIRIT AND THE CHURCH'S MASTER

DO we Christians have only the treasured memories of Christ as they are written down in a Book, or do we have the real presence of Christ as our divine Companion along the trail of life's going? The answer to that question, whether we are aware of it or not, brings us squarely up against the New Testament doctrine of the Holy Spirit.

"It is expedient for you that I go away," said Jesus to those perplexed and affrighted disciples of His. It is "to your advantage," is the way Weymouth translates it. "My going is for your good," is Moffatt's rendering. That He did go away is a fact well known to all of us. But how could He say that His going would be a good thing?

Frankly He could *not* have said it unless He had been prepared to assure them that His withdrawal in physical form was going to mean no grievous and gaping absence but rather His presence on a higher level. Earlier in this conversation He had said to them, "I will not leave you comfortless" (literally, "orphaned"). Now He assures them that the answer to their fears of loneliness will be found in the communication of the Holy Spirit. In this revelation Christ's presence will be experienced with a new and astonishing inwardness and intimacy. "He shall be in you," said the Master. "He shall abide with you for ever." He shall "glorify me." He shall "guide you into all truth."

Can anyone doubt that this was "good news" to those anxious and ill-equipped men upon whose ears fell the Master's words? Then it was, and is, what some have called the "gospel of the Holy Spirit." It answered certain vast and urgent needs that Jesus, more than others, understood in that hour of His approaching departure. What were those needs, and how does the Holy Spirit meet them?

I

The world must be gripped with conviction of sin: the Holy Spirit is the answer to that need. Consider the words that follow our text: "And when he is come, he will reprove the world of sin, and of righteousness, and of judgment: Of sin, because they believe not on me; of righteousness, because I go to my Father, and ye see me no more; of judgment, because the prince of this world is judged."

Someone ought to set up a "Bureau of Missing Words." If we had such an institution, somewhere on the dust-laden shelves would be found the word "sin." It is the forgotten word of proud twentieth-century man. We are so sure we have outgrown it that we would rather go to hell than to admit we are plagued with it. There is simply no end to the lengths we will go in building a silky vocabulary that leaves out the serpent-hissing word

—sin. The quack religionists are ready to lend a hand: they smilingly remind us that sin is merely a "delusion of mortal mind." The high-browed sociologists offer their assistance: they would sum up all that ails under the innocent-sounding phrase "the cultural lag." The super-patriots have a neat little suggestion too: they rise up self-righteously to declare that one or two madmen, like Hitler or Mussolini or Khrushchev are to blame for all this devilishness that has loosed itself upon the world.

The one thing that most of us are stubbornly unwilling to do is to locate the troubles of human society where they really are —inside our own prideful, peevish, perverse hearts, with their subtly persistent unbelief that turns away from God's Christ and serves other gods instead. Not long before he died in the period of the second World War the Archbishop of Canterbury said a thing that contains more moral insight and Christian wisdom than nine-tenths of the speeches and articles that are heard in Congress or published in newspaper columns. This terrible war, said Archbishop Temple, is simply "the latest, most violent manifestation of an all-pervasive element in the nature of unregenerate mankind." In other words, all of us are in on it in the measure that we have not allowed the redeeming Christ to save us from our self-centeredness, our callousness toward others, and our guilty failure to give God first place in our lives. It was the convicting Spirit of God that spoke through these plain words which the Archbishop uttered.

In the history of the Great Wall of China there is a parable of life that you and I might well take to heart. The wall was built for reasons of security. It cost a gigantic sum in money, time, and labor. Behind the completed barrier the Chinese people felt comfortably secure; yet in the first few years after it was finished it was breached three times by the enemy. But the thing to note is this: it was breached not by crashing the wall, but by bribing the gate keepers. It was the human factor that failed. The wall failed to work only because the men who guarded it failed. The material massiveness was insufficient; it needed moral character to support it.

It is time we listened to the Holy Spirit on this matter. We have built our walls, as individuals and as nations. We have put our confidence in scientific inventions, in mass education, in industrial and commercial organization, in political and social arrangements and, latterly, in military power and superiority. Everything has failed. Nothing we have tried has given us a happier and more secure world. Nothing will until we turn our eyes in the one direction where most of us do not want to look, which is right straight down into our own spoiled hearts where our dishonesties, evasions, sensualities, hatreds, and jealousies lie coiled up like so many red-tongued serpents with pretty designs on their backs but with deadly poison in their fangs.

It is *our* sin now—not our neighbors' or our ancestors' sin—but ours—which the Holy Spirit is dragging out into the light of honest day. It isn't murder, you say. Perhaps not. Only, remember that in God's sight and in the statement of God's Word "he that hateth his brother is a murderer." It isn't immorality, you say. Perhaps not. Only, remember that, according to Christ, there is an immorality of the voluntary thought-life which is equivalent to adultery. It isn't racketeering, you say. Perhaps not. Only, remember that "love is the fulfilling of the law," and a loveless heart, though it never go criminal, is before God only a gangster in evening dress.

So we may go on through the list of crimes from which we would fain excuse ourselves. But the Holy Spirit will not be put off so easily. Christ is not done with us until He has confronted us with this: "He will reprove the world of sin: . . . of sin, because they believe not on me." Call it the top sin, if you will, or the bottom sin; in any case it is the sin of sins, this refusal to bend low before Christ and accept Him as the "Immortal Love" who suffered, died, and rose again that He might bring us to God, forgiven and transformed. When the Holy Spirit has been allowed to grip us with this conviction, we shall be ready for our next step.

II

Christ must be glorified as a universal Saviour: the Holy Spirit is the answer to that need. Another area of the Spirit's activity, declares Jesus, concerns Me—My person and My work—"He shall glorify me" (v. 14). Joseph Parker, commenting on this phrase, makes the luminous remark that "what light is to the earth, the Holy Ghost is to Jesus Christ." And he adds, "The work of the Spirit is revelation, not creation. He does not make Christ, He explains Him."

As one aspect of this glorifying ministry of the Spirit of God, take the way in which He makes universally available the presence and the power of the Lord Jesus Christ. The historical Jesus, whom we meet in the gospel records, was confined within a human body. He worked within a human body. He worked within the limitations of time and space. He was on the Mount of Transfiguration with three fascinated disciples one moment, and at the foot of the mountain with a distressed father afterwards. He was not accessible in both places at the same time. He was in Galilee when His friend Lazarus died and in Judea, at the grave-side, four days later. He was not present in both places at the same time.

What was true of space was also true of time. Jesus lived thirty-three years. Suppose He had lived on in that body which He took to Himself through the mysterious process of the virgin birth. By the time He was five hundred years old, He would have destroyed His claim to be "made in all points like as we are, yet without sin." On the other hand, when He dies, rises again, and ascends into heaven, He must leave with men something more than the memory of His brief pilgrimage among them. Even that memory would cease to have any vivid meaning when death had removed the last man who had seen His face or heard His voice. Then we should have only a written record.

All of which argues eloquently for the Christian doctrine of the Holy Spirit. Only, be it noted, what we find in the New Testament is more than a doctrine—it is a series of glowing facts that are set on fire in the souls of men. We have, for example, Paul's profound insight. Christ, he says, "ascended up far above all heavens, that he might fill all things." "That he might fill all things"—all time, all space, all churches, all homes, all trusting hearts, all kingdoms and continents.

But how? Peter had the answer. He gave it to us on the day of Pentecost, when he, too, caught sight of the glorious plan by which Jesus of Nazareth was to swing out from the cramped boundaries of little Palestine and lay hold of the souls of men under every sky to redeem them to God. "Therefore," cried Peter, concerning His ascended Lord, "being by the right hand of God exalted, and having received of the Father the promise of the Holy Ghost, he hath shed forth this, which ye now see and hear" (Acts 2:33).

You ask, What is "the gospel of the Holy Spirit"? It is the gospel of Christ, the gospel of God's redeeming love, universalized. All men need our Saviour. All men may have Him— actually have Him in a living experience of His forgiveness and regeneration—through the Holy Spirit. All doors are now open. All barriers are down. All boundaries are overleaped. On a heathen temple in India is a sign which reads: "Low-castes and dogs not allowed." That is the exclusivism of paganism. It could even be found in Judaism in our Lord's time. Alas, misguided Christians sometimes duplicate it. But Calvary and Pentecost broke it forever.

And now what? In that same India it happened that one day a prominent Hindu woman came to a Christian worker. She brought with her a *devidasi,* a poor, bedraggled, abused temple girl. "I bring this girl to you to be saved," said the Hindu to the Christian. Then she explained, "I once heard my husband read a story from your sacred book, of a woman taken in adultery and what Jesus said to her and how He saved her. We have no such story in our books, so I bring the girl to you."

God be praised that we *do* have such a story in our sacred Book. But God be praised also that, because of the presence and ministry of the Holy Spirit, the story can be reproduced anywhere and everywhere, as aching hearts reach out with trusting hands to touch the Christ who died for them.

III

Christians must be graced with Christlike qualities: the Holy Spirit is the answer to that need. For, says Jesus, "he shall receive of mine, and shall show it unto you" (v. 14). In the light of these words we can agree with Schleiermacher that "the fruits of the Spirit are the virtues of Christ." According to Paul they are: "love, joy, peace, longsuffering, gentleness, goodness, faith, meekness, temperance."

Don't dismiss that list too lightly. Don't say, "Oh, well, every Christian has these graces in his life, and all he needs to do is to take time to develop them." That is just where some of us go clean off the track. True, all Christians have these qualities of Christlikeness more or less in evidence in their lives. True, also, these plants of spiritual beauty require time for full growth. But every gardener knows that if his soil is being taken by weeds or if his plants are not healthy, he needs something besides *time* to produce a lovely garden. Something drastic, like weeding or spraying, needs to be done. Then luxuriant growth and fragrant loveliness will follow in due course.

Pentecost came to the early Christians as a definite and drastic crisis in their career as Christians. "Suddenly . . . they were all filled with the Holy Ghost." They were searched, sanctified, humbled in one high hour of meeting with the Spirit of Christ. Other blessed hours followed, but this was decisive. It moved them over from the marginal waters to the central current of the stream of the Spirit. And all of this was somehow vitally related to a certain Christlikeness of disposition that they were normally to demonstrate.

Be sure of this, my fellow Christians: Any experience of the soul that makes us other than Christ-minded is not an experience of the Holy Spirit. It may be some other spirit—pride, hysteria, clannishness, sensualism—but it is not the Holy Comforter of whom the Master was speaking when He said, "He shall receive of mine, and he will show it unto you."

A friend of my father was one day addressing a body of ministers on "the fullness of the Holy Spirit." At the close of the message a minister came forward, deeply moved. His cheeks were wet with tears. He held one of the leading pulpits in that conference. "Your reading today broke my heart," said he, as he searched the face of the brother-preacher who had spoken. "I have been preaching Jesus, but I know I am not at all like Him. I have been cross to my wife, and to my children, and to my people. The past year has been a hard one; I cannot, I cannot try to preach Christ another year, unless I can have the 'mind' of Christ."

This, as it turned out, was the beginning of a short, sharp struggle within himself. Would he let go of himself and resign his whole being, his affairs, his future, his gifts, his family, into God's controlling hands? It was not settled easily, but it *was* settled. That day, and far into the night, the battle raged. In the small hours of the morning the flag of absolute surrender went up. The sovereign Christ, by the power of the Holy Spirit, took over. The result? Ask his wife. She testified to the new gentleness that was there. Ask his church officers. They testified to the new humility and winsomeness that were there. Ask his congregation. They testified to the new radiance and power that were there.

Here, it seems to me, in the everyday world of human relationships, is the kind of fulfillment that our Lord's promise of the Spirit requires: "He shall receive of mine"—my love and goodwill, my patience and peace, my compassion and courage —"and he will shew it unto you."

IV

The Church must be guided into all truth: the Holy Spirit answers to that need. Listen again to the Master in the context: "When he, the Spirit of truth, is come, he will guide you into all truth" (v. 13).

In whatever measure any man is honest with himself and his God, in exactly that measure does he long hungrily for truth. For in the realm of truth the mind and soul of man are in commerce with reality—the underlying reality that we may easily miss if we are occupied only with the facts that appear on life's surface. A botanist, analyzing a rose, gives you all of the dry facts about the stem, the stamen, the calyx, the petals, and all the rest. When he is through, you have something about as exciting as the multiplication tables. But the *truth* regarding a rose gathers up all the subtler things of form and fragrance and color and flings them into your beauty-ravished soul like a very gift of heaven.

Now it is the business of the Holy Spirit to make us lovers of truth and then to lead us into ever new and fuller appreciations of that incomparable One who is Himself the Truth. In Christ we have the Truth—the truth about God, the truth about man, the truth about sin, the truth about salvation, the truth about the meaning and goal of life, the truth about heaven, hell and destiny.

Does this mean that we know all there is to know about these matters that are so freighted with importance? Not at all. Christ gives the *key*. That key is in the hands of the Holy Spirit, and we, giving ourselves up to His guidance, are led into a progressive understanding of what it all means. The Spirit uses our minds; He stimulates our affections; He sharpens our intuitions; He enables us to interpret our experiences; He speaks to us through the testimony of others; He enriches us by the pooled wisdom of the whole community of believers. In all of these ways He is guiding us, slow and dull as we may be, into "all truth."

Let me add one word to that last sentence. Most of us Christians are much *more* "slow and dull" about spiritual realities than we should be. It is because we have never been to Pentecost for *our* invasion and inundation by the quickening, cleansing Spirit of God. The late Dr. Jowett looked at the early Christians before Pentecost and then at those same men and women after Pentecost, and he lifted his eyes to say that one of the differences which the fullness of the Holy Spirit made was "an extraor-

dinary power of spiritual apprehension." God was overwhelmingly real to them. Christ was so utterly dear and adequate.
Eternal things were so much more important to them than the
temporal. Prayer was so simple and natural. God's control of
their affairs was so close and continuous and all-satisfying. Life
was so radiant and conquering. And all of this in spite of in-
numerable privations, difficulties, and challenges.

They were being guided into all truth, and together they
were being used of God to guide others. Which is precisely
what the Church should be and do in this befogged and be-
wildered world.

The pilot of a "Flying Fortress" in World War II wrote to
a friend of his in Texas, describing the experiences he had in
bringing back his ship from many missions over Germany. He
was based in England. "A striking characteristic," he wrote,
"of an English landscape as seen from the air is the incredible
number of churches which the country boasts. These churches
have tall, stately spires and they afford excellent landmarks.
When the weather is bad, we use these churches as guides to
lead us home. We have become so familiar with them that when
we let down through an overcast and see a church beneath us,
we can immediately determine whether or not we are on our
course. Believe me, it is a very comforting sight to see them
appear out of the mists."

What suggestiveness in that sentence, "When the weather
is bad, we use these churches as guides to lead us home"! Ah,
my friends, in a far deeper and wider sense than that lieutenant
meant it, the weather of this morally befogged world *is* bad.
And the Church of Jesus Christ, under the guidance of the
Holy Spirit, is the signpost of the eternal God, pointing, ever
pointing, the way Home!

"*Come, Holy Spirit, come,*
    Let Thy bright beams arise;
Dispel all sorrow from our minds,
    All darkness from our eyes.

" *'Tis Thine to cleanse the heart,*
    To sanctify the soul;
To pour fresh life in every part,
    And new-create the whole.

"*Dwell therefore in our hearts,*
    Our minds from bondage free;
Then we shall know, and praise, and love
    The Father, Son, and Thee."

*"Ye are manifestly declared to be the
epistle of Christ ministered by us,
written not with ink, but with the
Spirit of the living God; not in tables
of stone, but in fleshy tables of the
heart."*

II 'Corinthians 3:3

8

THE HOLY SPIRIT
AND THE CHURCH'S MEN

IN the calendar of the Christian Church this is Pentecost
Sunday, which our British friends call Whitsunday.[1] The
churches generally do not make much of it—less indeed in the
United States than in Britain—but that is to their shame and
loss. It should be as heartily observed as Christmas or Easter.

The late Dr. J. D. Jones, of England, used to say: "There are
two things vital to the very existence of the Church—Easter
and Pentecost. Easter gave to the Church its gospel, Pentecost
gave it its power."

Easter is Christ *risen* on behalf of His Church. Pentcost is
Christ *released* within the very heart of His Church. Historically, we see this as we read the accounts given in the Gospels
and the Acts: Jesus telling the disciples that, following His
ascension, they would be empowered by the Holy Spirit (Acts

[1] This sermon was preached in First Covenant Church, Minneapolis.

1:8) and Luke recording how, on the day of Pentecost, "they were all filled with the Holy Spirit," how they witnessed miraculously in languages they had never learned, how the shackles of fear were struck from them, and how, with astonishing persuasiveness, they won thousands to the standard of faith in the crucified and risen Jesus which they had so boldly uplifted.

Great history, that! But if it is *only* history, then one feels like sighing, "Alas, alas, for the Church of the present hour!"

Thrilling to the story of the first Pentecost is one thing, stepping into the full stream of the Holy Spirit for oneself is quite another thing. *Admiration* for the men through whom the Spirit worked so mightily in the Book of Acts needs to be followed by *appropriation* of the selfsame Spirit for miracle-living in these stressful days. Today's observance of Pentecost will have remained in the shallows unless the abiding realities for which it stands are somehow brought home vividly and relevantly to each of us.

I

Let us begin by asking, What is the *message* of Pentecost?

It is this: Christ by His Holy Spirit becomes both resident and regnant in the individual and corporate life of the Church.

It is this: "Be not drunk with wine wherein is excess, but be filled with the Spirit."

It is this: "I came here a very important person, competent and smug. But I have lost my importance—in God." This was the witness of a Christian leader who attended a retreat where the Spirit-filled life was unfolded to him.

But now let us frankly face a barrier that stands in the way of this message regarding the Holy Spirit in the life of the Christian. There are numerous barriers, to be sure. This one, however, is basic. I have in mind the many who say that they have difficulty with the doctrine of the Holy Spirit *as a person*. Their attitude seems to be: We can grasp the doctrine of the Father and we can appreciate the doctrine of the Son, but we are mystified by the teaching that the Holy Spirit is as truly divine, as truly personal, as the Father and the Son.

One has sympathy with this perplexity, even though, on further reflection, the difficulty turns out to be less tough than we fancied it to be. I suspect that the Bible doctrine of God as Father is helped along in its appeal to our understanding simply by the fact that we have, ready to hand, a frame of reference within which to place it, namely, human fatherhood as we have known it in its finest flowering. "Father," as applied to God, is a figure, an image, that is concrete, familiar, attractive. We have known some wonderful fathers.

Similarly, Christ, the second person in the Trinity, although there is, admittedly, profound mystery in the inner relationship between the Father and the Son, represents something vivid and tangible. We think of Him as the man of Nazareth, who blessed little children, sympathized with the underprivileged, loved everybody, and finally died on a cross bearing the sins of the whole world.

But when we come to the Holy Spirit, we are suddenly left, we feel, without any definite thought-pattern into which we can fit Him. As compared with Fatherhood and Sonship, the idea of the Spirit seems unreal, illusive, impractical.

Perhaps we make the thought of the Spirit harder than it is. Actually it brings us closer to the essential nature of God than any title we use to describe the Deity. Did not Jesus say, "God is a Spirit, and they that worship him must worship in spirit and in truth"?

And is it not true that the most real and significant facts

about ourselves and our friends are the *spiritual*, that is, the immaterial, facts? Personality itself is spiritual. When a coroner examines a corpse he finds there everything physical that was present before. But he does not find your *mother* there, or your *wife*, or your *son*. The human spirit, the most meaningful reality about your dear one, is *not* there. Thus it requires only a little reflection to realize that *spirit*, so far from being unreal, is what makes possible in life and experience everything of value and beauty.

Transfer this thought to God, and see if it helps you to understand the personal intimacy with which God, as the Holy Spirit, seeks communion with your spirit.

Raymond Calkins somewhere suggests that all genuine Christian living has three—not one or two, but three—important and essential elements: There is the mind—we must have a reasonable belief in God; there is the will—we must be obedient disciples of the will of God as revealed to us in the example of Jesus Christ; but also we must be possessed of the Spirit of God; our whole natures must be filled with the very life of God, which so possesses us and fills us with its inexhaustible abundance that it transforms us from being weak and hesitating and tentative believers into bold, fearless, confident, conquering children of God.

It was precisely that which took place in the lives of the early Christians when, on that first Pentecost, they were brought so powerfully under the control and direction of the Spirit of God. Then it was that the Holy Spirit, as our text strikingly expresses it, wrote His own marks—which are, of course, the marks of Christ—upon them, not with ink, but with His own spiritual stamp. They became, in a new measure, "epistles of Christ," read and known of men.

II

What are the *marks* of the Holy Spirit in the life of the Christian?

(1) For one thing, He is known as the *Spirit of Truth*. In John 15:26 Jesus says: "But when the Comforter is come, whom I will send unto you from the Father, even the Spirit of Truth, which proceedeth from the Father, he shall testify of me." And in the following chapter occurs the statement, "When he, the Spirit of truth is come, he will guide you into all truth" (John 16:13).

Andrew Murray, in his excellent book *The Spirit of Christ,* has a chapter in which he reminds us of the two trees in the Garden of Eden—the Tree of Life and the Tree of Knowledge. Of the Tree of Life man was to eat, but not of the Tree of Knowledge. Now why Life before Knowledge? Because, as Murray puts it, "through life would come the knowledge and likeness of God." But man, falling before the sin of pride, put knowledge ahead of life, and his troubles began. They *began,* and they have not yet ended. For today, after the long story of proud man's effort to work out his own salvation, atomic man has the knowledge—the "know-how," as we say—to tap power that will blow him to smithereens, but he seems to have no secret that will enable him to live with that power, to live with his neighbor, or to live with himself.

All of which points up the towering claim of Jesus Christ as He comes among men with the offer of His salvation. First, we see in Him the blending of truth and life, the union of knowledge and goodness. Then we receive from Him the promise of this Spirit of Truth, the Spirit of the living God, who, as we yield to Him, will conform us to the image of Christ and give us insight into the nature of reality, into the message and meaning of Scripture, and into the glory of the unseen.

One of the distinctive things about a man who is sensitively yielded to the Spirit of Truth is that he does not take his orders from, or pattern his life after, the sometimes stupid, frequently shallow, and often pagan conventions and customs of the society in which he lives. He is *open* to truth.

Take the case of Peter in the early Church. He had been preaching to Jews only. Came a day, however, when he was invited to conduct meetings among the Gentiles in Caesarea.

He was on the point of saying No, feeling that the gospel was not for them, when the Spirit of God spoke to him: "What God hath cleansed, that call not thou common" (Acts 10:15). Then Peter flung his racial prejudice to the winds and began to fraternize with Gentiles in the ministry of Christ's universal gospel!

The same Spirit of Truth is at work today. I sat at lunch with a businessman in a Midwestern city and heard from his lips a story that, in some respects, duplicates the experience of Peter. This man, a deacon in a large church which is famous for its evangelical testimony, said that while the war was on, a Japanese *Nisei* applied for membership in the church. No one doubted the young man's conversion or the quality of his Christian life. Yet, when the application was presented to the board of deacons, that group of men was ready to turn it down. When the discussion revealed that the action, if taken that night, would be negative, the pastor moved to lay the matter on the table until the next meeting. Meanwhile the pastor conferred with his deacons. "What *Christian* grounds have we for rejecting this man?" he asked. They could think of none. When the matter came up again, a month later, the Japanese brother was received into the church, with nothing but the happiest results for all parties concerned.

Said that deacon, who shared the incident with me: "I used to feel differently on this race question, but the Lord showed me where my thinking was wrong."

That openness to truth is one of the marks of the Spirit of God. Upon our character and upon our behavior the Divine Spirit writes the holy script of the mind of Christ. Only thus can we become epistles of the living God to be read by all men.

(2) Again, the Spirit of God is known as the *Spirit of Holiness*. That phrase occurs in Paul's letter to the Romans where he speaks of Christ's resurrection as having been wrought by the Holy Spirit. "Jesus Christ," says Paul, was "declared to be the Son of God with power, according to the spirit of holiness, by the resurrection from the dead" (Romans 1:4).

For Christians there should be no serious problem over such blatant, easily labelled sins as lying or stealing or drunkenness. Most of us are all keyed up to denounce these evil things and willing to stay away from them.

But the Spirit of holiness in the Christian believer is never content simply to keep us out of such mischief. He searches and probes and convicts in those inner pockets of the soul where subtler evils lie. Take *pride*, for example. It is an infection of the carnal heart. If you want to detect it in yourself, catch yourself at the tendency to crave praise and flattery while you become depressed and irritated over criticism and disapproval. That pride needs to die, else the full glory of your Lord will never be seen in you.

Or that peevish temper, or that pushy, stubborn self-will, or that mean stinginess, or that smug complacency and lukewarmness of spirit—do you think that these are not sin in the eyes of God?

And do you think that the Spirit of holiness is not at war with these inner evils, rebuking them, exposing their real character, and asking for our believing consent to purge them away?

The trouble with too many Christians is that they are more concerned about their doctrine of holiness than they are about being clothed with the beauty of Christ's purity. Two Christian nurses fell into a heated argument over the doctrine of sanctification. One said that sin could be completely taken out of a person; the other denied it. Finally both of them lost their tempers, and both of them demonstrated that what they needed was not a *controversy* but a *cleansing*. They needed to make a full surrender to the Spirit of holiness. By so doing the stamp and image of Christlikeness would be written upon them and they, as epistles of God, would bear the message of His cleansing grace before the world.

(3) The Spirit of God, moreover, is the *Spirit of power*. To the disciples, just before His ascension, Jesus spoke two remarkable sentences that carried with them the promise of power. Luke records them both, one in his Gospel and one in the Acts. In Luke 24:49 our Lord instructs the disciples, "Tarry ye in the city of Jerusalem, until ye be endued with power from on high." In Acts 1:8 He assures them: "Ye shall receive power, after that the Holy Ghost is come upon you."

The word "power" fascinates most of us. In fact, ours is, to an extraordinary degree, a power-conscious and power-hungry age. Yet our conception of power and our use of such power as we have are so selfish, whether in the home or in international relationships, that we tend to wreck our world rather than save it.

Now go back to those early Christians and see what magnificent things happened to them when "the power of the Holy Spirit" took possession of them.

They experienced the ability, for example, to make Jesus Christ central in their lives. Before Pentecost Christ was in the picture, to be sure; but He was not steadily central. Think of Peter claiming in one hour that though all others might forsake Jesus, he would not, and the next hour trying to wriggle out of any connection whatever with the Master and His cause. What pitiable weakness!

Then look at Peter after Pentecost, standing up to face either a multitude or a bench of magistrates, and in any case bearing his unfaltering testimony to Jesus Christ as the crucified and risen Saviour.

Or think of the disciples at the Last Supper getting into an argument as to which of them was the greatest! After Pentecost that petty ambitiousness was lost completely in the passion of their ardor to exalt the Lord whom they served.

Certainly, it takes *power* to knock out the conceit and self-centeredness that have violated and marred our Christian discipleship, but such power is to be experienced any time we are ready to appropriate the promised fullness of the Holy Spirit. Power to make Christ central—can you think of anything in the Church today more desirable than that?

Speaking of the vast needs that challenge us in contemporary life, one writer observes: "Politics needs to be purified; our industrial world needs to be pacified; our social life needs to be simplified; our whole world needs to be unified." Granted! But how would it do to declare a holiday on all our grandiose schemes long enough to start something new. New? you say. O, yes, quite new! What is it? It is making Jesus Christ, actually and consistently, the Central Figure in our individual lives. If you don't think that takes *power,* it is because you have not seriously tried. It takes such power that only the Holy Spirit can furnish it. It is a major malady of our time that we want in the large what we are unwilling to adopt in the little. We want in the mass what we do not practice on the scale of the individual. We blame the United Nations for being so divided and futile when our homes are places of wrangling, of tension, and of frustration.

Power to make Christ central—how immensely we need it! Nor will it come by blowing on our hands and declaring that we are ready to turn over a new leaf. It will come when we kneel humbly before God in prayer. It will come when we Christians pray with faith: "Take us, Lord, O take us truly."

Then God will write the mark of power upon us and send us out as epistles of His grace to be read of all men.

III

What *measure* of the Spirit of God may we Christians expect and possess in order that the marks of the Spirit may be plainly and consistently seen upon us?

The answer is not difficult to find. Let us go back to the record of the first Pentecost: "And when the day of Pentecost was fully come, they were all with one accord in one place. And suddenly there came a sound from heaven as of a rushing mighty wind, and it filled all the house where they were sitting. And there appeared unto them cloven tongues like as of fire, and it sat upon each of them. And they were all filled with the Holy Ghost" (Acts 2:1-4).

They were all filled, that is, possessed, mastered, controlled!

We can have the Spirit of God in whatever measure we are willing and ready to give ourselves over to His occupancy and mastery. But let us not be confused by the word "measure." The Holy Spirit is neither a liquid nor a solid. He is a personality. When therefore we say in one breath that all Christians (all who in fact participate in the new life Christ bestows) have the

Holy Spirit and, in the next breath say that this is not necessarily the same as being filled with the Spirit, we are *not* talking nonsense. Even at the human level we recognize that inter-personal relations are of varying orders and degrees. A young lady by the name of Edith Brown began one day to exercise a more than ordinary influence on me. Our courtship became an engagement. I "had" her. She "had" me. We "had" each other. Yet I did not have her; not, at any rate, in the same manner or measure in which she became mine when we took each other at the marriage altar. The determinations and controls (and I must ask you to resist the facetiousness which I well know this word "controls" evokes) that she now exercised over my life took on a range of meaningfulness incomparably greater than I had known before.

Now move with me swiftly from that illustration by way of analogy to one that is drawn from the upper level of the Christian's relations with the Holy Spirit, or, if you prefer, his relations with the indwelling Christ *through* the Holy Spirit. Take the spiritual struggle and release that came to Oswald Chambers, whose well-known book of devotions, *My Utmost For His Highest,* is only one of many that came from his gifted pen. He was a philosophy tutor at Dunoon College. His trust in Christ as Saviour was sincere and unshakable. Equally unshakable, however, was the feeling that he was an appallingly dull, often defeated, sadly disillusioned sort of Christian. After four years of it, he was desperate. His language showed it. "I knew," he murmured, "that if what I had was all the Christianity there was, the thing was a fraud."

What marked the turn of the tide in this agonizing spiritual struggle was a visit to the College by Dr. F. B. Meyer and his Bible exposition on the subject of the Holy Spirit. It was a shaft of light in Chamber's heart, which was gray with gloom. "Luke

11:13," he tells us, "got hold of me—'If ye then, being evil, know how to give good gifts unto your children: how much more shall your heavenly Father give the Holy Spirit to them that ask him?' "

What was left of the struggle was brief but fierce. There came an hour of acute crisis: "Then and there I claimed the gift of the Holy Spirit in dogged committal on Luke 11:13." Result? Nothing that could be emotionally registered—no vision, no conscious power, no special God-realization, no witness.

The next step was that of going to a friend, and talking the whole thing out. Said the friend, "Don't you remember claiming the Holy Spirit as a gift on the word of Jesus, and that He said, 'Ye shall receive power . . . ?' "

"Then," says Chambers, "like a flash something happened inside me, and I saw that I had been wanting power in my own hand, so to speak, that I might say—Look what I have by putting my all on the altar!"

Five years later Chambers could set it down: "If the previous four years had been hell on earth, these five years have truly been heaven on earth. . . . The last aching abyss of the human heart is filled to overflowing with the love of God. Love is the beginning, love is the middle, and love is the end."

Now, suppose we ask, Had the Holy Spirit no place in Oswald Chambers' Christian life up to this time of deeper crisis? Of course, He had. Who but the Spirit had shown him Christ as a trustworthy Saviour? Who but the Spirit had sustained within him this sometimes faltering trust? Who but the Spirit had even used him to bring others to a living experience of Christ?

What then had taken place? Never mind the incidental matters—the shockingly desperate terms in which the soul's hunger and dissatisfaction were described, who preached the convicting sermon, what passage of Scripture came alive for him, and all the rest. What centrally happened seems to be this, that the Spirit of God, already his, got his believing consent to take the actual, total control of his life and to make meaningful the claims of Christ's lordship which from the day of his conversion had been authentically there.

This is what Sam Shoemaker, in his recent book on the Holy Spirit, describes as stepping from the marginal waters of the spiritual life into "the stream of the Spirit." Masses of us Christians seem never to take this step. Many who do fail to remain in the stream. But none of us has a right to say that *living* there, *abiding* there, *abounding* there, is not our privilege.

Besides, let it be plain to all of us that no crisis, however searching or significant, is a substitute for the ensuing process of growing and maturing. One must say, in the language of a verse I once discovered in a sermon of Stuart Holden's:

> *"There are heights of sweet communion that are all*
> *   awaiting me,*
> *There are ocean-depths of mercy that are flowing*
> *   full and free;*
> *There are precious pearls of promise that can ne'er*
> *   be priced in gold,*
> *There's a fulness in my Saviour that has never yet*
> *· been told."*

With what measure of the Spirit are we content? Let that question come home to us now. Some Christians act as if their prayer to the Holy Spirit is: "Please, a minimum of interference with my life!" God forgive us!

Who is ready to fling such an unworthy prayer to the winds and replace it with a worthier one—even this: "Please, Holy Spirit, a maximum of control over my life!"

As God is my witness, I know of no other way by which these lives of ours can be made to bear the signature of Jesus Christ. I know of nothing short of the Spirit's control that will enable Him to make a tablet of you and me, and on that tablet write those living characters which, when read by other people, make them think of Jesus Christ.

"But ye shall receive power, after that the Holy Ghost is come upon you: and ye shall be witnesses unto me both in Jerusalem, and in all Judaea, and in Samaria, and unto the uttermost part of the earth."

Acts 1:8

9

THE HOLY SPIRIT AND
THE CHURCH'S MISSION

IF there is anything that completely misses the nature and spirit of the Christian gospel, it is the idea that this good news of Jesus Christ as Saviour and Lord can be kept bottled up —bottled up in somebody's cozy soul, bottled up in somebody's sectarian group, bottled up in somebody's already gospel-privileged country.

World War I, when thousands of American soldiers fought against the autocracy of the Kaiser, made America conscious of *Europe*. World War II, when scores of thousands of GI's fought along the farther shores of the Pacific, made America conscious of *Asia*. By then we began using a word that was new to us—the word "global." For the first time in history man's military inhumanity to man was witnessed literally on a world-wide scale.

But let us never forget that the Christian Church has been

globally minded for two thousand years—at least when she has been truly the Church.

Our Lord put the "glow" and the "go" into the word "global." "Go ye into all the world, and preach the gospel to *every creature*" (Mark 16:15).

"Go ye therefore and make disciples of *all the nations*" (Matthew 28:19, ASV).

"Ye shall be witnesses unto . . . the *uttermost part of the earth.*"

"Every creature."

"All nations."

"The uttermost part of the earth."

There, clear as a beacon in the black, is the original missionary impulse and imperative. This is the Church's mission, and if she is not carrying it out, it is her fatal omission.

I

Let me speak first of the *source* of this impulse to world missions as we have it in the text. Consider these words: "the Holy Spirit . . . upon you."

In Luke and John the giving of the Great Commission is directly associated by our Lord with the person and work of the Holy Spirit in the believer.

You will recall Luke's account: "And [Jesus] said unto them, Thus it is written, and thus it behoved Christ to suffer, and to rise from the dead the third day: and that repentance and remission of sins should be preached in his name among all nations. . . . And ye are witnesses of these things."

Then what? "And, behold, I send the promise of my Father upon you: but tarry ye in the city of Jerusalem, until ye be endued with power from on high" (Luke 24:46-49). If anyone doubts that the "promise of my Father" is a phrase referring to the Holy Spirit, let him take serious notice of what the Lord says in the setting of our text: "being assembled together with them [He] commanded them that they should not depart from Jerusalem, but wait for the promise of the Father, which, saith he, ye have heard of me. For John truly baptized with water, but ye shall be baptized with the Holy Ghost not many days hence" (Acts 1:4, 5).

Or, take the version of the Great Commission that we have in John. "As my Father hath sent me, even so send I you." Then what? "And when he had said this, he breathed on them, and saith unto them, Receive ye the Holy Ghost" (John 20:21, 22).

No wonder that Andrew Murray, himself so deeply immersed in the things of the Spirit, has said: "Missions are the typical work of the Holy Spirit. No one may expect to be filled with the Spirit if he is not willing to be used for missions."

Let the question now be faced, Are we as Christians *struggling along* pretty much on our own in the life we live and the work we do, or are we being *carried along* on the released flood of life which God makes ours "after that the Holy Spirit is come upon you"? That is not conversion. It is Pentecost!

I have heard it argued that *all* Christians have the Holy Spirit and that therefore it makes no sense to teach some subsequent experience of the Spirit. Have such persons, who reason thus, forgotten that our Lord Jesus had the Holy Spirit during all those growing-up and maturing years at Nazareth? Have they forgotten that when at the age of thirty He entered upon His public ministry the Holy Spirit came upon Him?

The *philosophy* of it is not as important as the *fact* of it— either with Jesus or with you and me.

II

If the *source* of the missionary impulse is the Holy Spirit, what may we say of its *force?* The answer speaks strongly from our text: "Ye shall receive the *power* of the Holy Spirit."

Study the Book of Acts, and you will find that this power exhibits three outstanding aspects: the power of *cleansed personality*, the power of *unified community*, and the power of *confident adequacy*.

The Spirit-possessed men and women of the Acts had undergone a spiritual purging. "Their hearts were purified by faith," as Peter puts it. They had been radically cleansed—cleansed of their selfish ambition for place and preferment, cleansed of their resentments, cleansed of their self-righteous pride, cleansed of their crippling fears.

Just as surely these Christians of the Acts, when Spirit-filled, were amazingly welded together in a working fellowship. "They were all of one accord" is the verdict of chapter 2. "They were all of one heart and one soul" is the declaration of chapter 4.

Before Pentecost they worked *under* a strain, and it was mischief; after Pentecost they worked *on* a strain, and it was music. They might be pressured and persecuted from without, but they were held together in a living fellowship within.

With equal certainty we can say that these mission-minded early disciples displayed a sense of adequacy, an undiscourageable invincibility, which again and again turned back their enemies.

Oddly enough, they had no confidence in themselves. Nobly enough, they had boundless confidence in the risen Lord who was using them to His glory. Hence they could say, looking unflinchingly into the angry eyes of their persecutors: "We ought to obey God rather than men."

The echoes of that unbeatable confidence are still heard.

Listen to Mary Slessor, the Scottish girl who pioneered for Christ in Africa. When an African chief, listening to her proposals of what she would do, blurted out, "You, you do all of this? Why, you are only a woman!" she replied, "Yes, but you have forgotten the woman's God!"

Listen to David Livingstone, set upon by wild beasts, stricken by one attack of African fever after another, still saying, with dauntless courage: "I will go anywhere, provided it is forward!"

How do you account for these things? Let us take the rest of the quotation from Andrew Murray: "No one who wishes to work or pray for missions need fear his feebleness or poverty: the Holy Spirit is the power that can fit him to take his divinely appointed place in the work."

III

Let me speak, finally, of the *course* of the missionary impulse. If its *derivation* is from the Holy Spirit and its *dynamic* is the Spirit's power, its *direction* is that of world-wide witness. "Ye shall be witnesses unto me both in Jerusalem, and in all Judaea, and in Samaria, and unto the uttermost part of the earth."

I have an abridged dictionary on my desk. Under the word "witness" it says: "be evidence; give evidence." I like that. "*Be* evidence!"

One way we Christians can witness is just by our *stand*. What we *are* is as truly vocal as what we say. The convictions we hold, the attitudes we display, the high sense of duty by which we are moved, the thousand little acts of every workaday week— these make us magnets by which people are drawn to our Saviour. The biographer of Henry Drummond said that writing the story of his life was "like writing the history of a fragrance." How eloquently that speaks of the Christlike soul of the man!

I know a missionary in India whose life and spirit had so impressed a "sweeper"—the lowest of the low among the many castes of that land—that he one day said to the missionary: "You come and walk through the humble compound of my cottage, and it will be purified of all its impurities and inferiorities." With characteristic humility my friend said: "I knew his faith was misplaced; I couldn't do that. But I knew Jesus could do it." The point is that my friend's living example had made the poor man feel that the former could do what in fact only the Christ he represented could do. When you and I live like that we are witnessing with an authentic Christian witness.

Furthermore, in carrying out the missionary impulse we are to witness by our *stewardship*. Turn but a page or two in this thrilling Book of Acts, and you find these Spirit-intoxicated Christians laying all their possessions at the feet of Jesus Christ and at the disposal of His Church. In chapter 4:32 we read: "neither said any of them that ought of the things he possessed was his own."

How much there is of Christ in the economic life of today is an open question. One thing is sure: the economics that most students study and that most Americans practice is not the same as Christian stewardship. Stewardship is partnership with our Lord Jesus Christ in the possession and use of material goods. As one of our most thoughtful advocates of stewardship puts it, "Economics says of things: these must satisfy *man*. But stewardship says of things: these must glorify *God*."

It is that difference of approach that makes the difference between the materialism of Christianity and all other materialisms. Professor Charles Malik, of Lebanon, calls it "spiritualized materialism." For let it be perfectly clear: Christianity *is* materialistic. It asserts a material world. It teaches a material body.

It gives place in its view of the future to a "resurrection of the body."

Yet all of this materialism it affirms *spiritually* by making man the owner of none of it, but rather God. Man is a tenant and trustee, whom God will hold accountable for the use of this world's goods in such a way that the ends of His Kingdom are served and not strangled. When the United States can spend nearly four billion dollars a year for tobacco, and nine billion for liquor, and approximately a billion and a half for jewelry, it clearly suggests that it has no serious sense of stewardship, no solemn fear of offending the God who expects us to make material goods the instruments of His Kingdom.

By contrast, let me point to a contemporary sample of stewardship. The name of Lillian Thrasher means nothing to most of us. Yet she is one of the most famous women of the Middle East. Up to the time she was sixteen she had never seen a Bible. Shortly after giving her heart to Christ, she was in a quiet woodland one day. She had picked some flowers. Overwhelmingly the thought came to her: "How much I owe to my Saviour! I want to give Him something." She prayed: "Lord, I do wish I had something to give Thee, but I have nothing but these flowers." So, having nothing else, she presented them to Him, and with them herself.

In 1910 she landed in Egypt as a missionary. One day she was at the bedside of a dying mother, who was trying to feed her baby from a tin container. The milk had become green and stringy and partly caked. The mother gave Lillian her baby, and died. That was the beginning of an orphanage that has been going for over forty years.

It started when Lillian rented a little house for $12.50 a month, and put her own little savings into furnishings for it. People from all over the world have given to that orphanage.

A Scottish nobleman, a member of the House of Lords, has given over $35,000.00. When Miss Thrasher, with some embarrassment, asked him how she should address a nobleman of Scotland, his reply was: "Address me any way you like. Any titles I may have shrink to insignificance before the nobility of your character and work."

They call her "The Nile Mother." When Jerome Beatty wrote her story for the *American Magazine,* he said: "Egypt is the land of wonders, but to me its greatest is Miss Lillian Thrasher." This was a missionary impulse translated into stewardship!

Something else belongs to the course pursued by mission-minded Christians: they witness, as we have seen, by their stand, by their stewardship, and also by their *speech.*

When the day of Pentecost came and these men and women who first heard the words of our text were filled with the Holy Spirit, something happened to their characters, to be sure, but also something happened to their conversation. Besides finding a new vitality and a new victory, they found a new *voice.* They "began to speak with other tongues [or languages], as the Spirit gave them utterance" (Acts 2:4).

In their case there was an actual physical and psychological miracle: they spoke instantly and for the occasion in a variety of languages and were understood without an interpreter by the representatives of many different language groups who were present. That outer miracle may or may not be repeated. What is repeated, wherever Christians surrender themselves fully to the Holy Spirit, is the inner miracle of the bold and happy witness.

Today the Church has largely lost its witnessing voice. If it speaks, it speaks through official pronouncements by bishops or printed resolutions by conferences and conventions. That is not what we mainly need. We need hosts of Christians, in every walk of life, every club and every craft, every parlor and every plant, who are so full of the love and power of Christ that they do not simply wait for an opportunity to talk about their Saviour. They wisely seek and guidedly make opportunities.

Sam Shoemaker says to today's Christians, "You can't stop a runaway world by keeping still!" Correct! Evil advertises. Sin is articulate. Unbelief is vocal. Communism is loudly aggressive. A silent Church is no match for all of this.

Some of us Christians have been in the Church a long time, but we have never given our tongue to the Holy Spirit. This we have never done because we have never really and unreservedly given ourselves over to Christ's lordship. Hence we are always offering excuses for our unexpressive, non-communicating faith. We are too timid, or too uninformed, or too old, or too busy—and on it goes!

The real fact is we are not overflowing with the Spirit. One wise leader has said, "The depth of an experience of Christ may be measured by our inability to keep still about it." If he's right, a lot of us are paddling around in the spiritual shallows.

Here is the example of a church lady. She had been brought up in the church. It was a church, however, where the minister did practically everything and the laymen were expected to be quietly docile and pay the bills. One day she met a minister of her own denomination whom the Holy Spirit had set on fire. She told him she wished she had what he had, but was sure it was not for her. These excuses were given between puffs on her cigarette. But later the spiritual miracle hit her. She was "born again." She dedicated her life to the business of witnessing. God's Holy Spirit possessed her, mastered her, made her exuberant. A friend of hers reported: "I just had a telephone call from her. . . . She's incurably cheerful, gay as a lark, a transformed personality in Christ, witnessing day by day to employees, guests, friends, about what has come into her own life."

There you have it—a description of the missionary impulse in action! It is the same today as it was in the Church of the first century. In principle it is the same in Africa as it is in America, the same in Mombasa as it is in Minneapolis!

"Ye shall receive . . . !"

Have you?

IV

"TO THE GREAT ONE IN THREE"

"Holy, holy, holy, Lord
  God of hosts, eternal King,
By the heavens and earth adored!
  Angels and archangels sing,
Chanting everlastingly
To the blessed Trinity.

"Thousands, tens of thousands, stand,
  Spirits blest, before Thy throne,
Speeding thence at Thy command,
  And, when Thy behests are done,
Singing everlastingly
To the blessed Trinity.

"Thee apostles, prophets Thee,
  Thee the noble martyr band,
Praise with solemn jubilee;
  Thee, the church in every land;
Singing everlastingly
To the blessed Trinity."
                    —CHRISTOPHER WORDSWORTH

*"The grace of the Lord Jesus Christ,
and the love of God, and the communion of the Holy Ghost, be with
you all. Amen."*

II Corinthians 13:14

10

WHAT DO WE PREACH ON TRINITY SUNDAY?

A distinguished radio preacher from Australia asked a cele-
brated radio preacher in America what questions of
faith seemed to be most perplexing or disturbing to people. The
American minister's reply was: "The Trinity and the Virgin
Birth."

The Christian belief in the Trinity—Father, Son, and Holy
Spirit in the unity of the one Godhead—may be heavy with
mystery when it is in the hands of the theologians, but in the
heart of the Church it is light and bright with music. The
mystery is there, to be sure. It will always be there. Yet it is the
kind of mystery without which the Church finds that it is *not*
the Church.

The human experience of love is not less real because it holds
at its heart a mystery that turns mathematics into a mockery.
A mother, for example, has three sons. She writes a letter to each
of them. She ends each letter by saying, "I send you all my

107

love!" And she means it. Let a mathematician try to square *that!*

Our text gives us, mystery and all, what is commonly called the "Apostolic Benediction." The word "Trinity" is not used. Nevertheless, out of this and similar passages in the New Testament the Church, fortified by its own Christian experiences, has developed what we know as the doctrine of the Holy Trinity. For this reason, too, we have in the Church Year what is known as Trinity Sunday.

I

Let me bring forward the first of several questions that I want to raise and attempt to answer: *Why a Trinity Sunday?*

Let us begin by recalling certain Christian facts—just the bare facts, with no attempt, now, to explain.

We might start with the fact that when the risen Jesus gave His followers—the Church—their marching orders for the long years ahead, He said, in part: "Go ye therefore, and teach all nations, baptizing them in the name of the Father, and of the Son, and of the Holy Ghost" (Matt. 28:20).

Here is a second fact. For more than fifteen hundred years great masses of Christians in many communions have been repeating a statement of their faith called the "Apostles' Creed." In that creed the Church says: "I believe in God the Father, Almighty . . . and in Jesus Christ his only Son our Lord. . . . I believe in the Holy Ghost."

Another fact: the Westminster Catechism, used by Presbyterians and others in the Reformed tradition, after asking the question "How many persons are there in the Godhead?" answers, "There are three persons in the Godhead, the Father, the Son, and the Holy Ghost; and these three are one God, the same in substance, equal in power and glory."

Still another: the American Book of Common Prayer in its revision of 1928, used by the Episcopalians, contains a Doxology which reads: "Let us bless the Father, and the Son, and the Holy Ghost: praise Him and magnify Him forever."

And· yet another: the Book of Worship of the Methodist Church contains this prayer for Trinity Sunday: "O Eternal God, Father, Son, and Holy Spirit, grant that in the majesty of all creation we may behold Thy power that upholds us, in the face of Jesus Christ Thy love that seeks and saves us, and in new life within our souls Thy Spirit kindling in us; that so even to our littleness Thine infinite wonder may be revealed, O blessed Triune God. Amen."

And, finally, consider the fact that you, and millions of your fellow Christians with you, have sung again and again:

> "Holy, holy, holy, Lord God Almighty!
> All Thy works shall praise Thy name,
> In earth, and sky, and sea;
> Holy, holy, holy! Merciful and Mighty!
> God in three Persons, blessed Trinity!"

Now, however you and I may personally feel about this matter, the reason for Trinity Sunday is that the Church—or great sections of it as least—felt the need of a day when it would call upon its members to reaffirm the faith that has been passed on to them concerning the triune God. It should be a day when some helpful teaching concerning the Holy Trinity is given to the people and when they, on their part, join meaningfully in worship as they bow before the everlasting mystery of Father, Son, and Holy Ghost.

II

We come now to our second question, which I venture to raise bluntly in this form: *Why a doctrine of the Trinity anyhow?*

I shall try to give you three answers to this query:

Because, for one thing, *nothing short of this three-personal God does justice to the experience of the early Christians.* There are two mistakes into which people have fallen at this point. One is the mistake of imagining—for it is fancy and not fact—that the Christian belief in the Trinity was originally the cunning work of some theologians who got their heads together and said, in effect, "Let us compose a doctrine that says there are three Gods which nevertheless add up to only one God!" If any of you have come across that notion, I'd like to tip you off: Don't fall for it unless you happen to be one of those persons who love to be fooled. Mind you, I am not saying that the theologians did not get into the "act" at all. They did. But that, in the main, came later.

The other mistake is that of imagining that Christianity began with what some people—including some scholars—are fond of calling the simple teacher of Galilee, Jesus, and the simple experience of following Him that came to the first disciples. The facts are, of course, that Jesus was not the simple peasant teacher that these over-simple people try to make Him, nor was the experience of Jesus that came to the first Christians as clear and uncomplicated as these friends would have us believe.

I am perfectly willing to join any man in saying, "Away with needless mysteries and complications!" but I am not willing to close my eyes to the fact that many phases of reality are mysterious to the point where no one can ever completely explain them. When people try to get simpler than life itself, they are in danger of becoming simple fools.

Now what was the experience of God that unfolded in the lives of the first Christian believers? It was so new and tremendous that it shook their thinking to the foundation. It broke some old molds and shaped up some new ones.

Don't forget that these early Christians were first men who had been steeped in the faith of the Hebrews that there is one God. They believed *that,* and believed it passionately. The pagan notion of many gods was a horrible thing to them. They were, what we call, technically, "monotheists"—one-God worshippers.

But see what happened to them! Jesus of Nazareth came amongst them, called them to be His friends and companions, lived sinlessly in their presence, performed miracles before their eyes, gave them such insights into life and reality as they had never received from anyone else, claimed to have come from a previous existence with God through all the eternity of the past, declared that He would give His life for the sins of the world, went to a cross where His enemies appeared to have disposed of Him, rose from the dead the third day, and began again His thrilling communications with His disciples.

What could these disciples do when they faced, as they had to face it, the question, *What manner of person is this Jesus?* Did they give up their faith in the God of the Hebrews, the One sovereign Creator and Lord? No. Did they add Jesus to their religion as a second God? No, there is no reason to believe they did.

What they did was to accept and confess a mystery—a mystery which nevertheless they could not deny. They were compelled to make room in their thinking for an understanding of God that was bigger than they had previously imagined it could be. The Father in heaven is God; Jesus of Nazareth is God; and the two are so related that in Jesus God actually "comes through," incarnates Himself, unveils Himself as the God who *acts* for man's salvation. Hence the confession of the first Christians: "Thou art the Christ, the Son of the living God" (Matthew 16:16).

But we are not finished with that Christian experience of the original Christians. The risen Jesus went away. He "ascended into heaven," as the Apostles' Creed puts it. Then came Pentecost and the invasion of the lives of those early disciples by an inward sense of God's presence so real and so gripping that they said to one another, "This is it! This is what Jesus told us it would be—the coming of the Holy Spirit in a deep dimension of inwardness. This is more than just a kindling of our memories of Jesus. This is greater than a hero-worship that leads us to idealize a lost leader. This is the risen Saviour given back to us in the personal presence of the Holy Spirit. This, too, is God!"

When you remember that the coming of the Holy Spirit did not lead them for one moment to think of a third God, but rather made them more sure than ever of the Fatherhood of the God they had always believed in and the Saviourhood of the Christ they had so recently come to know, you begin to realize what I mean when I say that these Christians had a trinitarian *Christianity* even before they had a trinitarian *theology*.

So it is not too much to say that this Christian experience, big, and full, and revolutionary, forced upon apostles like Peter and John and Paul the development of the conviction of the Trinity. I could have said the "development of the *idea* of the Trinity," but that sounds too much as if they were spinning theories. They weren't. They were interpreting their experience under the illumination of God's guiding Spirit.

God the Father: *for* us in love, eternally!

God the Son—*with* us in grace, historically, but also eternally!

God the Holy Spirit: *in* us in power, experientially, historically, and eternally!

This, then, is our first answer to the question, Why a doctrine of the Trinity?

Move on to a second answer: *because nothing short of this God-in-three-persons does justice to God.* For example, Christians believe, following the Apostle John, that "God is love." Suppose you ask, "How long has He been love?" I doubt if you ever met a Christian who would not reply, "Always!" Now "always" is a big, long entity. God loves His human creatures, but there was a time when there wasn't one of them to love. God might be said, though awkwardly, it seems to me, to love His material universe. But there was a time when not one bit of star dust was in existence. Can God love when He has no object to love? Did He perhaps just love Himself? Perhaps, but does that not strike a false note?

Now there is another alternative. What if God is in fact a unity of three Persons? Then there is, in the rich plurality of the divine oneness, a society—an eternal social structure—in which Father, Son, and Spirit bestow affection and satisfaction on one another. I am not saying that this conception is without mystery. I am content to say that with all its unprobed depths of mystery it still says something wonderful about the eternal nature of love that we affirm of God.

And may I add this: if you deny the trinity of God, you have no room to account for all the liberty and variety which God shows in history with regard to His movements and actions. You have no *real* way of explaining the deity of Christ, the humble, crucified Jesus. You have no *real* way—a way, mind you, that goes beyond mere words—of accounting for the actual presence of God within the consciousness of the living Church and the individual believers who make up the Church.

We should not be afraid of this diversity in God—this three-personed activity of His. In other realms unity is combined with plurality. The much publicized atom of the modern world is a tiny, amazing unity, but scientific man has learned that it can be divided, and it can be divided because it is a diversity that subsists within unity. The government of the United States is one government, but it exists in plurality, with the *legislative,* the *executive,* and the *judiciary* separate and distinct, yet one. And I would defy you to take any one of them away without abolishing the government of the United States *as a republic.*

Argument from analogy is not always safe, I know; but I find it hard to escape the conclusion that if you take away from the conception of God the truth that speaks in the word "Father," or the truth that speaks in the word "Son," or the truth that speaks in the word "Holy Spirit," you do not have left the Christian God. And it is the Christian God I want.

And now a brief word about the third reason for a doctrine of the Trinity. I have said that anything less than such a faith fails to do justice to Christian experience and fails to do justice to God. Let me now say that *it fails to do justice to the permanently inspired record of the New Testament.*

Quickly I must warn you that you will not find a deliberate or systematic setting forth of the Trinity in the New Testament, just as you will not find a systematic argument for, or explanation of, God in the Old Testament. What you will find, however, is a consistent set of propositions and insights that make abundantly clear the trinitarian position of the New Testament Church.

I have already cited Matthew's account of our Lord's instruction: "baptizing them in the name of the *Father,* and of the *Son,* and of the *Holy Ghost.*"

Add to that the record by John in the Fourth Gospel, chapter

14:16 and 17, where Jesus is quoted as saying: "I will pray the Father, and he shall give you another Comforter, that he may abide with you for ever; even the *Spirit* of truth."

Add to that the statement by Peter in Acts 10:38, "*God* anointed *Jesus* of Nazareth with the *Holy Ghost* and with power."

And, to remind you of only one more passage, there is the magnificent trinitarian benediction with which we began: "The grace of the *Lord Jesus Christ,* and the love of *God,* and the communion of the *Holy Ghost,* be with you all."

It is never enough to say that the triune God has revealed Himself in (1) acts of history or (2) in realities of experience. It is necessary to add that He has revealed Himself as Father, Son, and Spirit *through the Biblical writers who have authoritatively recorded and interpreted the saving acts of God in history.*

III

And now our concluding question: *Why preach on the Trinity?*

In order to clear up the mystery of it? That will never be done. Mystery there will always be, as there always should be.

In order to engage in speculative theological discussion? That is not reason big enough for a sermon.

The answer, I think, is in our text. It is because my *heart* needs, even as yours does, the "grace" of Christ, the "love" of God, and the "communion," or "fellowship," of the Holy Spirit.

My heart needs the "grace" of Christ. It is the grace of which St. Paul speaks elsewhere: "Ye know the grace of our Lord Jesus Christ, that, though he was rich, yet for our sakes he became poor, that ye through his poverty might be rich" (II Corinthians 8:9). I am a bankrupt. I stand before God poverty-stricken. But Christ in grace goes surety for me, supplies the spiritual capital on which I begin the real business of living. One of the ladies of our church gave me one day a definition of grace that she had heard years ago: "The grace of Christ is help for the helpless, hope for the hopeless, and everything for nothing!" That is it!

But my heart needs the "love" of God too. It needs to know that the gracious act of Christ's dying for me was not just an isolated episode in which a heroic man did his best for me. My heart needs to know that the Cross is the work and the pledge of the sovereign God of heaven and earth. It is a sampling of the love that beats forever at the heart of the universe, which is the heart of the Father-God.

And surely my heart needs the "fellowship" of the Holy Spirit. This I take to mean the community of Christians who by the Holy Spirit are all infused with God's life and are in love with God's Christ. This is the Church—God's own new creation. It is the fellowship in which the needs of all are the concern of each and the burdens of each become the care of all. It is the company of Christly souls that has become the speaking lips, the seeing eyes, the toiling hands, the marching feet, the burning heart of Jesus Christ—and I need it.

Grace, love, fellowship . . . Christ, God, the Spirit—my heart needs it all, embraces it all, worships because of it all.

Horace Bushnell, in the early years before he became the great preacher he was, was a tutor at Yale. Brilliant, restless, religiously perplexed, he came at last to spiritual assurance through a profound surrender to Christ. Later he confessed to his fellow tutors:

"When the preacher touches the Trinity and when logic shatters it all to pieces, I am all at the four winds. But I am glad I have a heart as well as a head. .My heart wants the Father; my heart wants the Son; my heart wants the Holy Ghost—and one just as much as the other. My heart says the Bible has a Trinity for me, and I mean to hold by my heart."

Some of the rest of us mean to also!

> *"Hallelujah! Lord, to Thee,*
> *Father, Son, and Holy Ghost,*
> *Godhead one, and persons three,*
> *Join we with the heavenly host,*
> *Singing everlastingly*
> *To the blessed Trinity."*